FUNDAMENTALS OF DIRECTING

FUNDAMENTALS OF **DIRECTING**

BY **RIC KNOWLES**

WITH ILLUSTRATIONS
BY **PAT FLOOD**

PLAYWRIGHTS CANADA PRESS
TORONTO

Fundamentals of Directing © 2015 by Ric Knowles

LIBRARY AND ARCHIVES CANADA CATALOGUING IN PUBLICATION
Knowles, Ric, 1950-, author
        Fundamentals of directing / Ric Knowles ; illustrated by Pat Flood. -- First edition.

Includes bibliographical references and index.
Issued in print and electronic formats.
ISBN 978-1-77091-470-4 (paperback).--ISBN 978-1-77091-471-1 (pdf).--ISBN 978-1-77091-472-8 (epub).--ISBN 978-1-77091-473-5 (mobi)

        1. Theater--Production and direction. I. Flood, Patricia, illustrator II. Title.

PN2053.K56 2015   792.02'33   C2015-904089-2
                                            C2015-904090-6

We acknowledge the financial support of the Canada Council for the Arts, the Ontario Arts Council (OAC), the Ontario Media Development Corporation, and the Government of Canada through the Canada Book Fund for our publishing activities. Nous remercions l'appui financier du Conseil des Arts du Canada, le Conseil arts de l'Ontario (CAO), la Société de développement de l'industrie des médias de l'Ontario, et le Gouvernement du Canada par l'entremise du Fonds du livre du Canada pour nos activités d'édition.

Canada Council   Conseil des arts
for the Arts   du Canada

ONTARIO ARTS COUNCIL
CONSEIL DES ARTS DE L'ONTARIO
an Ontario government agency
un organisme du gouvernement de l'Ontario

Canada

Ontario
Ontario Media Development
Corporation

For Christine

CONTENTS

FOREWORD
BY NINA LEE AQUINO

I find it funny that I'm writing this foreword.

The title of this book is the same as the title of the course I took in my third year at the University of Guelph. I was at a crossroads in my theatre life at that time; I'd been pursuing theatre training as an actor and it wasn't quite working out. After a number of rejections from university productions (including one directed by Ric himself), I decided to take a break and pursue anything *but* acting. Which is how I found myself in a class called Fundamentals of Directing.

Directing was something that was outside my range of interests—I really didn't think I had it in me—I only took the class because there weren't any others to take, seeing as I'd just retired from acting. I had no idea that a schedule-filler would end up changing the course of my artistic life.

I don't know for certain if you can learn how to direct by taking a class or by reading a book, but I'm inclined to say you can't. Fundamentals of Directing wasn't so much about *what* Ric taught but *how* he taught it. Similarly, this book is not meant to tell you how to direct. How you see the world of the play and how the characters inhabiting it operate is entirely up to you. But to be given guideposts on how to start thinking about things as a director is invaluable. God knows, everyone needs a guidepost every now and again to clue us in to where might we go next . . . or at least to get our bearings checked at a pit stop somewhere along our creative process.

Really, the key requirement for learning how to direct is the simple act of doing it. And there's no other way to try out what's outlined in this book. So you've just got to do it: really direct a play. For real. And then, if you're fortunate enough to get another opportunity to direct, take that one. Do it and keep doing it. Simple as that. The whole vision spiel and talking about what you want to do on stage—those are important things to communicate but they don't exist until you're actually in the thick of it. That's when you get to know your process, your artistic sensibilities, your aesthetic, your visual style, your own directing lingo, and even the kinds of works (text or non-text creations) you're attracted to. You need to dive right in, headfirst.

Even then, with all the experience you will gain from the practice of directing, your directorial process shifts with the kind of play you decide to take on. There is no one-size-fits-all in directing. There are, however, a couple of things that always hold true no matter what kind of play you end up helming. This book helps you think about those constants. Call them what you like: guideposts, prime directives, points of light. They help directing become . . . not so directionless. Or overwhelming. Or scary. And I guess that's what I love most about the course and this book.

Fundamentals of Directing doesn't have the singular "know-it-all" tone that other books about directing (at least from my experience) normally carry. Ric offers perspectives from his own experiences as a director, but he also shares other directors' processes from observing them at work in the rehearsal room or from direct collaborations with the multitudes of productions he has worked on. I have to admit to being a touch overwhelmed that I'm one of those people captured in this book. I still don't know how that happened. One minute I'm in Ric's class trying to figure out what I want to do with my life and the next I am struggling to write a foreword for his book *that is* all about my life.

Ric's course—and, now, this book—reminds directors that we're not alone in doing this work. There are other key players. And this is, I think, one of the most important things I learned from him as my mentor: direction is the art of collaboration and being able to communicate the fruits of that collaboration. A director is a master collaborator, expertly juggling the choices and offerings from a creative team, actors, and even producers. Filtering all of that, sifting through and letting it all influence, affect, or confirm your beliefs ultimately allows you to make the best directorial choices possible. You're allowing the people around you to do what they're supposed to do, allowing them to offer up their gifts to the vision, thus making everything fuller, multi-layered, complex, and rich.

A collaborative process means you're free to imagine the world in all its senses—sight, sound, feel, taste, and touch—and your creative teammates get the pleasure of transforming those senses into reality without the burden of thinking about exits and entrances or spotlights and gobos; or leather or latex; fades in and out.

This book gives you the tools to imagine a backbone or an interesting skeleton to which the meat and the muscles and even the heart (because often times you won't find that right at the beginning) hang on to. And after the seeking, the exploration and discovery; after the creative back and forth of jam sessions and the collaborative decisions . . . what you've got is a full-bodied production. A unique beast moving, shifting, transforming on the stage, teeming with life and vitality.

You know, like every show out there should be.

PREFACE

I've been teaching a twelve-week practical introductory course on theatre directing at the University of Guelph for twenty-five years. This book, a distillation of what I've taught, is intended to focus on and outline what the title shared by the course and the book calls directing's "fundamentals." It's intended in part as a textbook, and if used as such it should be read in conjunction with practical labs and workshops on the topics of each section, in which students flex their own directorial muscles in the studio and learn from their mistakes.

This book is also intended as a guide for aspiring directors from all sorts of contexts—the conservatory, the academy, community theatre, and of course its primary target, the profession, where, again, it should be read in conjunction with as much practical, hands-on apprenticeship and application as possible. Directing can't be learned from a textbook alone.

Fundamentals of Directing assumes some familiarity on the part of its readers with what actors, designers, stage managers, and technicians do, assumes that readers have been through at least one or two rehearsal processes at some level and in some capacity, and assumes some familiarity with the vocabulary of the stage.

It's organized for the most part to reproduce the chronology of a rehearsal process, beginning with brief and general background information on the history and varied practices and positionings of directors. It then moves through the various stages of a directorial process from selecting a project through auditioning, working with designers, actors, and technicians to closing night.

This chronology, however, doesn't play itself out in practice as cleanly as in theory, and many things that are described in these pages as discrete steps usually overlap or even develop simultaneously: directing is in many ways the ultimate art of multi-tasking. I recommend, then, that the book be read through in its entirety before returning to reread it section by section and to do practical exercises around each section in sequence. Following the book section by section through the stages of a rehearsal process would also be appropriate.

Although the immediate context from which the book draws its examples and situates its advice is the professional theatre in Canada, it applies without much slippage quite broadly to amateur and academic theatre, to community theatre, and to theatre outside of Canada. I hope that teachers, students, and aspiring directors will find it useful.

ACKNOWLEDGEMENTS

This book owes its existence to my earliest mentor and teacher as a director, Robin Phillips, who claimed he didn't know how to teach directing. I'm also deeply indebted to all of the directors, designers, actors, and technicians with whom I've worked over the last thirty-odd years, and from whom I've learned everything I know about directing. I'm indebted in a different way to all of those students in my Fundamentals of Directing classes at the University of Guelph since 1989 for forcing me to come to whatever clarity I have about the subject. I'm also indebted to Nina Lee Aquino, Thomas Morgan Jones, Clare Preuss, and Guillermo Verdecchia, from whom I've consciously stolen; to the many others from whom I've learned and stolen unconsciously; and to Nina, Thom, Guillermo, Tony Berto, and Yvette Nolan, who told me I had to write this stuff down and publish it. Nina, Thom, and Yvette also read drafts of the manuscript and helped to make it better, as did my friend and colleague Harry Lane, the best teaching director I have encountered over the course of my career.

As always, my deepest debts are to Christine Bold, to whom this book, like all my work, is dedicated.

INTRODUCTION

Although all cultures have practised a variety of performance forms throughout history and prehistory, "theatre," as it's known in the western world, is a western invention, and the director, a figure that we today find so essential, has only existed as such since the late nineteenth century.

The role of the director emerged in theory through Richard Wagner's concept of the *Gesamtkunstwerk* ("total work of art")—a synthesis of the poetic, visual, musical, and dramatic arts as espoused through a series of essays between 1849 and 1852; in practice it emerged through the influence of the Duke of Saxe-Meiningen, whose company toured Europe in 1874 winning admiration for its unity of vision, for the careful coaching of everyone involved, and for its focus on the ensemble.

There was, of course, an approximation of some aspects of the director function in Greek theatre (where the playwright oversaw production and trained the chorus), in medieval theatre (where a pageant master—a kind of managerial role—oversaw staging), in early modern through nineteenth-century European and North American theatre (where an actor-manager ran the company and cast the shows), and in the performance forms of many non-western cultures.

But the invention of the position of director *as creative artist* coincided with the late nineteenth- and early twentieth-century birth of modernism in Europe, with its focus on such things as unity, generic purity, individual artistic vision, and the concomitant concept of "genius." But unity, generic purity, and individual vision have often been associated with a prescriptive, sometimes even a fascist politics. Are they always desirable objectives in a collaborative art form?

There are two dominant approaches to directing in today's theatre training, both of which are problematic: the director as absolute leader, general, visionary, and authority, the sole source of wisdom, creativity, insight, and power; and the director as chairperson, coordinating a democratic "journey of exploration and discovery."

I prefer to think of directing as a process that positions the director as neither of these things. I think of directing as a collaborative process in which the director serves as a focal point for the project and provides a clearly defined *context* within which all of the collaborators work as contributing artists, producing a whole that is more than the sum of its parts and more than what any individual director might have imagined on her or his own.

The director, in my view, is neither absolute leader nor merely chairperson, but is responsible for coordinating a process that consists of a series of choices, each one of which becomes part of the context within which subsequent choices are made. The director is ultimately responsible for these choices, though s/he may or may not be the one who makes them. The director's "vision" is what initiates and guides the project, but the director is not the sole source of wisdom and inspiration, which can come from anywhere.

There are two other, related issues to consider, if only to set them aside: the director as interpreter (an exegetical role) and as *auteur*. I don't believe in the former, which establishes a text (usually an already written and completed script), and therefore its author, as final authority. I consider the text to be not "the play" that is "realized" through performance or subjected to interpretation (or deconstruction) by directors or theatre companies but as one (and only one) of the resources that may (or may not) be brought to bear collaboratively on a theatrical production, with no more authority than any other. In my view "the play" does not exist except in its reception by specific audiences at specific performances of specific productions. "Dramatic literature" is a different genre entirely, one which has its interest and uses, but one that has little to do, except theoretically, with theatrical production.

On the other hand, I don't believe that it's productive to think of the director as *auteur* in the collaborative art form that is the theatre. I believe that the precise role of the director will be determined by the project and the team that's assembled to carry it out, as well as by the personality and self-positioning of the individual director. Above all, however, directing is about *communication*:

1. *Within the creative team*. It's essential that everyone working on a production be in constant communication with one another, and it's up to the director to know *how* to communicate with each of

the production's designers, actors, technicians, stage managers, producers, and so on—which means cultivating as full a knowledge as possible of each of these disciplines *and* their specialized ways of speaking, thinking, and working.

2. *Between the stage and the audience.* A show's meaning and impact are produced collaboratively between the creators and the audience, and it's within the audience that a production has its impact. A director has to be constantly conscious of what a production's communicating, who it's speaking to, and what it's saying to or performing upon them.

An aspiring director needs to ask: What kind of director do I want to be? Why do I want to direct? Why theatre? What do I want to *do* as a director?

1. SCRIPT ANALYSIS

I've argued that theatre is not about the interpretation or staging of scripts, which I consider, when they're part of the process (as we'll see in Appendix B, they aren't always), to be simply one among many of the resources used in staging a production. But when they are used, like each of the other resources, they need to be subject to systematic directorial analysis well before casting or consultation with other collaborators can begin. This is true whether the script is treated as primary, providing the fundamental dramaturgical architecture of a production (as in new or recent plays that are not in the public domain), or whether it goes through various kinds of de- and reconstruction over the course of rehearsals and the show's structure derives from other principles or considerations (as is sometimes the case with classical scripts).

But first there are some preliminary, reflexive questions that need to be asked. These have to do with the initial selection of a script and the reasons for undertaking the task in the first place—the *need* for you as director to undertake this particular project at this particular place and time for this particular audience.

I find it useful to consider the staging of a production to be research and to begin with a research question, an attempt to understand or make sense of something that's urgent. Every script brings with it different imperatives, and every director must bring her or his own positioning to bear on each analysis s/he undertakes. A script analysis begins by asking "what do I want to know? Why do *I* want to know it? Why now? What key issues will the production explore? Why does it matter? To whom does it matter?" The greater the urgency of the question, as a rule, the more important the production will be.

I also find it useful to phrase the question and design the process under the assumption, to quote playwright and director Yvette Nolan, that "maybe if we can work it out in this play, we can work it out in our lives too."[*]

There are many elements of a script analysis and many languages through which a script speaks, and each of these requires careful and detailed consideration, both separately and in combination with one another. But first I find it helpful to engage with the script as directly as possible, to read it through at a single sitting, without interruption, note-taking, or analysis. Only after completing the reading, and perhaps after an interval, do I take random and usually unsystematic note of first impressions and, most importantly, visceral responses. It's important throughout the process to be able to return to these notes as a record of what first seemed powerful, compelling, important, or intriguing about the script.

After an interval of perhaps a day or two, I find that a second reading can productively test those reactions. Do they still hold up? What different aspects of the script drew attention

---

[*] Yvette Nolan, "*The Death of a Chief*: An Interview with Yvette Nolan," interview with Sorouja Moll, *Canadian Adaptations of Shakespeare Project*, 7 July 2006, http://www.canadianshakespeares. ca/i_ynolan2.cfm. Accessed 11 July 2013.

the second time around? I tend to repeat this process as often as it continues to seem valuable and until I feel I have a good generalist knowledge of the script and have notes about everything that the script evokes for me: images, thoughts, ideas, colours, shapes, sounds, associations, connections to other work or to the world and to that of the audience. At this stage it's important that these notes not involve specific ideas about staging; if they do, this can pre-empt productive negotiations with designers and other collaborators that raise the level beyond what any of you individually might have envisioned.

The next stage is to read for analysis, beginning with the overarching questions of *what, for you, the script is about* and *how this is communicated*. This is in part a process of selection: no script, and no production, can be about everything, and at least initially you're concerned with primary meanings that you feel are foregrounded by the script. It's important to consider what your *central* concern is, what (based on your initial readings and subsequent analysis) you want to foreground as primary, and what other meanings exist that play a contextualizing, supporting, or complicating role.

It's similarly the case that *how* the play's meanings are communicated involves a wide range of interrelated languages and techniques. Part of the process of your analysis is to decide what, for you, the play's *primary modes of communication* are: does it work chiefly through character? plot? action? imagery? dialogue? gesture? Most scripts use all of these and more, but your decision about which, for you, is (or are) primary allows you to consider what drives the play and how each of the others relate to it.

If a play's primary mode of communication is character, does the plot put the characters into situations that reveal, challenge, modify, or undermine them? Is character revealed through the give-and-take of dialogue, through monologues (or soliloquies), through the way the character speaks (her choice of words and images, his syntax, their rhythms or silences)? Or is it revealed through action, what the characters actually *do*, which may or may not reinforce or undermine what they say (or what is said about them)?

If plot is foregrounded, is there a hero or perhaps an unlikely central character or characters (or other forces) as primary pressures driving the story? I tend to think of a play as an assemblage of "what ifs?" that are thrown together in strategic combinations in order to see what happens as they interact. Many of these "what ifs?" are embodied in characters, but others might be ideas, social conventions, weather, or other forces brought to bear on the action.

The World of the Play

Once you've determined what, for you, the play is about and what its primary modes of communication are, it's useful to begin with an analysis of what is somewhat loosely called "the world of the play." One aspect of this analysis is to determine the play's overall poetic and imagistic vocabulary and resonances, which can usually reveal whether the play participates in a society dominated by culture, nature, economics, politics, sports, and so on, and whether this can be realized in performance through design and staging.

At least as important as the play's imagery, however, is its logic. Naturalistic drama, because it sets out to investigate the cause-and-effect "laws of nature," including human nature, attempts to follow the logic of the "real world" and to make visible its workings. But much theatre operates by different rules entirely, often establishing its own conventions, and it's essential that any script analysis determine what these rules are, how and when they are established, and the relationship between the represented world they regulate and that of the audience. Sometimes this is as simple as agreeing that asides and soliloquies, heard by the audience, can't be heard by other characters occupying the space, or that a few armed extras rushing across the stage represent two warring armies, or that walls exist that are manifestly not there.

Understanding the play's explicit or implicit structuring of space can in fact be central to the analysis of the world of a play. This can mean simple things like understanding what offstage spaces are imagined in relation to the place or places represented on stage—that the offstage left door leads to the lake, the upstage door to the bedroom, and so on, and eventually how this might shape blocking, movement, and design. It can also mean more complex analyses of how the script structures the relationships between characters, between characters and places or spaces, or between representational and non-representational playing spaces. Fundamentally, a script analysis considers how a script imagines space; its degree of restrictiveness, compression, or capaciousness; and how it organizes social relations and orchestrates movement. For a more complete discussion of the spatial aspects of a production see Section Nine.

Part of the logic of any play world are what Konstantin Stanislavski called its "given circumstances," and it's essential that you as director identify what these are so that everyone working on a production is on the same page. Given circumstances include such things as where and when the action is taking place; how old the characters are; what their relationships are to one another at the outset; what their social, cultural, and economic backgrounds and statuses are; and anything else that we know about them and the world they live in. Some of these are usually clearly discernible in a script's stage directions or dialogue, but some scripts—notably most of Shakespeare's plays and those of his contemporaries—have little indication of them and they have to be decided upon. It's a significant problem in rehearsals if one actor assumes the action is taking place on a cold and rainy October evening in Moscow in 1865, and another that it is a hot summer afternoon in Winnipeg in the present—particularly if the designers have another idea entirely.

Sometimes a play world operates by laws that are entirely different from those of the "real world," or the world of the audience, with (for example) space being compressed, stretched or reconfigured according to the play's idiosyncratic physics, or with time being elongated, compacted, or reversed.

It's also helpful to consider closely what Elinor Fuchs calls "the social world of the play," asking such crucial questions as "who has power on this planet?"* Sometimes this is obvious (the king), sometimes less so, particularly if the action

---

* Elinor Fuchs, "EF's Visit to a Small Planet: Some Questions to Ask a Play," *Theater* 34.2 (2005): 7.

is set in small-town or unfamiliar societies where particular histories and sensibilities can create and sustain unpredictable power differentials. These have to be uncovered and made clear through dramaturgical analysis.

In plays that invoke the supernatural it's necessary to determine how much power, say, the witches in *Macbeth* actually have, whether and when they can intervene in the daily life of the characters. When is a *deus ex machina* the logical and satisfying outcome of the action and when is it a monumental cop-out? In adaptations of Franz Kafka, in Eugène Ionesco, or in Samuel Beckett, when is the play's twisted or absurd logic a productive commentary on the bureaucratic or absurd rules that seem to govern "real-world" experience, and when is it just silly (or Absurd)?

What are the spiritual or cultural belief systems, epistemologies, and cosmologies that underscore the action in culturally specific work? When the Rugaru (an ominous figure in Algonquin cosmology) appears in Algonquin playwright Yvette Nolan's *Annie Mae's Movement*, what is its ontological status? When a large half-naked Native man appears as an answer to Grace's prayers in Nolan's play *Job's Wife*, who *is* he, and what relationship does he bear to the world of the audience?

Intertextuality

A thorough script analysis needs to take into account the ways in which a script may not be self-contained. This involves, at a minimum, identifying intertextual references (references to other work, other genres, other realms), intended or otherwise, that open the world of the play into the realm of the social. This means tracking down moments in a script that cite works of art, ideas, theories, historical figures and events, or social movements, and analyzing their function within or beyond the script. It means researching those references in an attempt to understand what ways of thinking they invoke, what contrasts or similarities they provoke, and what larger ideas they introduce to the play.

One of the prime functions of intertextuality is to frame audiences' expectations. Recognizing the discourses and conventions of a particular genre, for example, audiences can have their expectations either satisfyingly fulfilled or productively disappointed, but as a director you have to know what those expectations are in order to shape them to your purposes. Original audiences for Shakespeare's *King Lear*, for example, would have recognized that the play follows the structural conventions of comedy and is based on a familiar (to them) older play, *King Leir*, which had a happy ending. Unlike audiences today shaped by the expectations of Shakespearean tragedy, they would have been surprised and devastated by the entrance of Lear with his daughter Cordelia dead in his arms.

Modes: Narrative, Lyric, and Dramatic

Many approaches to the study of writing, including the typical course offerings at schools and universities, divide the discipline into genres: poetry, fiction, non-fiction, and drama. This division has its uses. What it often fails to take into account, however, is the fact that each of these genres employs what I think of as different modes (rather than genres)—the narrative, lyric, and dramatic, all of which can appear in a single work in any genre:

> 1. *The narrative mode*, quite simply, has a story and a storyteller. Much of the interest in most narratives is in the relationship between the two and the degree to which the reader, listener, or audience trusts the narrator or shares her perspective. Narrative carries with it an element of pastness, of events already complete, always already told and retold.
>
> 2. *The lyric mode*, on the other hand, while it also has a "storyteller"—at least insofar as it has a presenting voice—it has no story in the traditional sense: it is generally concerned with description, expression, and the evocation of an emotional response. It, too, can evoke the past—there is an element of reflection in much lyric writing—but it also conveys emotion that is "present-ed" (or made present).

3. The third, *the dramatic mode*, has a story but no storyteller: the story is *shown*—the basic element of theatre. It has a sense of immediacy, and the audience is left to its own devices to determine the story's meaning.

Narrative is most frequently associated with novels, short stories, ballads, and historical non-fiction—each of which, nevertheless, can contain (dramatic) dialogue and lyrical moments of pure description or expression. The *lyric* mode is most frequently associated with lyrical poetry and song "lyrics"—which often, of course, emerge from an implicit or incipient situation or "story" and which can also include dialogue. And of course the *dramatic* mode is most frequently associated with plays.

But most plays, while relying principally on the dramatic mode, employ all three, sometimes sequentially, sometimes at a single moment. In Shakespeare, soliloquies often lyrically and eloquently express the state of mind of Hamlet, Macbeth, Lear, or Othello, while direct address by messengers such as the Captain reporting on the battle in the second scene of *Macbeth*, or by choric figures in *Pericles* or *The Winter's Tale*, functions as pure narrative. The chorus in *Henry V* might be understood as a narrator explicitly lamenting the limitations of the dramatic mode while stepping in between the acts to fill the gaps.

Always the modes function and acquire meaning relationally, and it's important to identify as part of a script analysis what mode is at work, when and how these modes contribute to the play's functioning, how they shape its rhythms, how the shifts from one predominant mode to another occur, and how they vary the script's textures.

Backstories, exposition, and gaps can be filled in through the use of narrative, for example, while varying the mode of address. Similarly, the immediacy and forward thrust of dramatic action can pause and be reflected upon in lyrical passages. But lyrical and narrative moments within a naturalistic (or any) play need to be handled carefully, because they can shatter the illusion or shift the terms of engagement in ways that require attention and awareness. This is why it's so difficult for many directors to find ways of dealing with the famous soliloquies in Shakespeare, when lyrical expression trumps action and the audience gets a window into the characters' souls.

Signs: Iconic, Indexical, and Symbolic

Theorist Charles Peirce has identified three different types of "sign"—three different ways in which one thing can represent, or stand for, another, and his differentiation is useful for script analysis.

1. The first type he identifies is the "*iconic*" sign, in which the relationship between the sign and what it stands for is based on resemblance. A chair on stage "stands for" or represents a chair in the fictional world of the play. An actor (a human being) represents a character (also a human being).

2. The second type of sign Peirce identifies is the "*index*," or "*indexical sign*," in which the sign *points to* what it stands for. A road sign points the way to a city, a knock on the door points to the fact that someone is there, smoke points toward the existence of fire, words such as "his," "hers," "this," or "that" point gesturally to someone or something that is only legible in the moment.

3. Peirce's third type of sign is the "*symbol*," where the relationship between the sign and what it stands for is arbitrary, but is agreed upon by convention. Most spoken or written language works symbolically, there being no logical relationship, for example, between "cat," written or spoken, and a four-legged furry mammal that meows and purrs. The word functions as a symbol—but not all symbols are words.

Theatre relies heavily on resemblance, on the iconic mode of signification. But just as there are lyrical and narrative moments within the predominantly dramatic mode of most scripts, so there are indexical and symbolic signs within a type of writing, the dramatic, that relies predominantly on iconicity. If on the stage a "real" chair stands iconically for a chair in the play's fictional world, it might also, if set amongst a row of chairs, with magazines, point indexically to an offstage doctor's office. Or it might operate symbolically (by convention) as a rock or platform on which people climb to look over a wall.

It's important in undertaking script analysis to recognize when a sign evokes its referent

1. *Iconically*, through resemblance, and therefore refers to meanings already available (the audience recognizes a chair on the stage as the sign of a chair, or of a throne, within the fictional world);

2. *Indexically*, through indications or pointings that establish their meaning in the here and now (a character exits to go to what she indicates is in the garden, or threatens someone she refers to as "you"); or

3. *Symbolically*, through arbitrary or unmotivated assignations of meaning that project into a future (the script assigns a meaning to a phrase or object—"the Grinch," perhaps—that the audience will subsequently understand as symbolic of envy, or lack of empathy, or meanness).

Iconic signs—whether they be painted backdrops, real furnishings, or actors playing characters—can most often be easily read and recognized, but can also be least interesting for an audience familiar with the unchallenged theatrical conventions of the moment.

Indexical signs can require more effort for a director or an audience member, working out where "here" and "there" are; who or what "you" and "she" or "this," "that," and "there" refer to; and just what the dialogue or action is pointing to off stage or outside of the timeframe of the action. Most scripts require careful attention to such signs, and some instances— such as King Lear's famous last words, "Look there, look there!" (V.3.312)—are ultimately ambiguous or even enigmatic and require directorial decision-making: as an ungrounded indexical sign, Lear's "there" is up for directorial grabs.

Symbolic signs, finally, require either insider knowledge (membership in the community that has assigned them meaning), translation (for non-members of that community), or participation in the script's own establishment of a henceforth shared (or shattered) convention: "This castle," Duncan says, presumably pointing to the upstage tiring house in *Macbeth*, "hath a pleasant seat," and we agree, for now, on where we are (Shakespeare, *Macbeth* I.6.1).

Iconic signs are particularly useful in naturalistic theatre, where resemblance between the sign and its referent works to invite an audience's recognition and therefore admits them to the world (and incorporates them into the ideology) of the play: "yes, that's a chair"; "yes, I recognize that actor with the curly blond hair and short skirt as an attractive young woman."

The use of an indexical sign, however, can disrupt the taken-for-grantedness of this recognition—"look, isn't *that* strange?"; "how could something like *that* happen?"; or "how did *that* representation—curly blond hair and skirts—become a sign of female attractiveness?"

The sign as symbol, particularly when it insists on its own arbitrariness, can create the possibility of new and emerging languages and meanings, the opportunity for directorial invention, but also for failure to communicate to an audience that may not understand the codes.

Structure: Plot and Character

Structure simply refers to how the script is put together. This involves analyzing, as it would for the structural analysis of a bridge:

1. Its materials (what it's made of),

2. Its design (how those materials are arranged), and

3. How these materials and their arrangement relate to its function.

In the case of a bridge, it would be surprising if a footbridge over a stream were to have the same materials or design as a bridge for cars, trucks, and trains that also has to leave room for cargo ships beneath. The materials for most scripts are all or some of: plot, characters (or roles), action, and language, though there are many other materials (such as images) that can dominate in certain types of script. Most scripts are organized in time and space through the use of acts, scenes, exits, entrances, or other units.

A structural analysis involves identifying the units, what they are made of, what's in them, how they relate to one another, and what those relationships serve to communicate. A detailed script analysis involves breaking the play up into units and identifying what happens in each unit, exactly where and how the audience learns exactly what information, and at exactly what points significant changes occur.

Many actors, and many directors, have learned to break individual scenes down further into *beats*, units within the scene in which a single action occurs. This can be useful, particularly when starting and stopping scene work in rehearsals. But beats are nebulous things; not all scenes function through isolatable units of action that are determined by the script and that apply equally to all actors, and most actors will find different beats in a single scene. I find it more useful to work with actors on "thought units," which are not determined by the script and which apply to individual actors only, as discussed in Section Eleven.

Plot

Plot consists of the organization and presentation of the story. It's useful when analyzing plot to distinguish it schematically—even mechanically—from the purely chronological story. Indeed, it's often useful to go so far as to map the story chronologically from beginning to end, beginning with the first thing that happens, and mapping it against the plot, when it is revealed or represented.

The earliest events in the story are not, in most cases, where the *plot* of the play begins, which is often *in medias res* (in the middle of things), sometimes even at the end, proceeding through flashbacks and skipping over periods when "nothing happens." Many plays, from *Oedipus Rex* to *A Doll's House*, turn on the revelation of actions that precede those depicted on the stage. Arthur Schnitzler's 1897 play *La Ronde* uses a kind of relay structure, in which one character only from each scene carries on into the next, temporal "development" imitating the round dance after which the play is named. Judith Thompson's *Lion in the Streets* employs a similar structure. *Same Time, Next Year*, by Bernard Slade, involves two characters, each married to others, meeting once a year for twenty-four years for an affair, with the "action" of the play primarily involving their discussion of what happens between their meetings. Colleen Murphy's *The December Man* begins at the end and moves chronologically backward to the story's beginning.

Each of these and many other structures shape and are shaped by what the plays are setting out to do and what meanings they're attempting to convey. In the case of *Oedipus*, the focus is on consequences; in the case of *A Doll's House* on realizations; and in the case of *The December Man* (which deals with the so-called "Montreal massacre," in which thirteen engineering students and one staff member were murdered because they were women)—or virtually any work that begins with the end of the story—the focus is not on "what happens next?" but on "why did this happen?" or even "how could this possibly have happened?"

It's essential in a script analysis to determine the initiating action in the plot—the action or event that introduces what the play will be about—and what the final action is, when the play's exploration of that subject or issue is complete (or strategically left open).

It's the initiating action at which the structural analysis of any script begins. Such an analysis will then identify the various units, however defined, that together constitute the script, considering what these units consist of, how many of them there are, how they relate to one another, and what patterns and shapes they establish. A unit can be an act or scene as indicated in the script; a "French scene," which begins and ends with any entrance or exit; or any other analytical division that serves to structure the action.

An analysis of structure will consider such things as what new information is introduced to the audience in each unit, the points at which the action changes direction, and the shape of the script as it evolves. It's often useful to spatialize plot structure by charting it on a graph, with act, scene, and line numbers marking where significant events occur that change the course of the action. And it's useful within this to consider such things as which and how many characters (or other "dramatic postulates" that put pressure on the action) are present in each scene, what forces they bring to bear on one another, and how these forces play themselves out.

It's also useful to map the temporality of the represented action against the "real time" of the audience and to chart the action's pace and rhythm. There is an identifiable music in every script, moving (with identifiable rhythms) through various crescendos and diminuendos, through various keys, and from various atonalities and dissonances to varying degrees of harmony or (ir)resolution. I often map these rhythms and cadences by actually "drumming" through the play's units to get a sense of exactly where the play's rhythms are regular, when they are syncopated, when the tempo waxes and wanes, when dissonance resolves itself into harmony—and each of these, again, can be mapped on a graph, or even on a musical score. All of this work eventually pays off, not only in work with composers and sound designers, but especially in rehearsal with actors (who may, however, have different or better versions of the same exercise).

Character

Character analysis in most English-speaking contexts, particularly for those trained in the Stanislavski System or American Method and their variants, is generally understood to consist of mining the script for clues about the characters' psychological depths, motivations, and objectives. In naturalistic plays this usefully consists of considering carefully not simply what a character says and does, what is said about them, and the tensions among these, but also how the character speaks.

Considering how a character speaks means, first, analyzing their *word choice*: what worlds do their words come from? Are they Latinate, sophisticated, and abstract, for example, or are they folksy, colloquial, and earthy? A character who refers to "automobiles" can reasonably be understood to come from a different social and psychological realm than one who talks about "cars" and another who refers to his "wheels." Characters from different realms will talk about "excrement," "doo-doo," and "shit."

Similarly a character might draw her *imagery* and figurative language from the corporate, legal, political, academic, artistic, medical, sports, or natural worlds. Much is revealed when different characters talk in different metaphors about the bottom line, the finish line, the outline, or the line on the horizon.

Syntax can be similarly revealing. A character who speaks in long, convoluted sentences with multiple conditional clauses is easily distinguished from one who speaks in short, simple sentences. A prevalence of interrogatives (questions) reveals a different cast of mind than do declaratives (statements) or even imperatives (commands). "Would you like to come in and have a seat?" is very different from "there are lots of places to sit," or from simply "sit down."

Similar analyses can be done of a character's individual rhythms (short and clipped, long and languid, regular or irregular) and even of their preference for voiced or unvoiced consonants, or for short or long, close or open, front or back vowels. In Henrik Ibsen's *A Doll's House*, Torvald's "is my little lark twittering out there?" with its short "i" vowel sounds and its labial "l" consonants is a world away from the world-weary long vowels and voiced consonants of Mrs. Linde's "nine, ten long years."

This psychological and linguistic character analysis has to be supplemented by a consideration of the characters and other elements in the play (including abstractions, collectives, groups, things, and offstage pressures) as *forces* that are brought to bear on the action and on one another. These forces, when they *are* performed by the characters, are usefully distinguished from Stanislavskian objectives and super-objectives because they operate on the level of plot rather than of motivation and because any one of them can simultaneously or sequentially bring different things into play.

The forces at work in any script can be psychological, social, cultural, ethical, political, or ideological, and they can enter the force field of the action through character, collective, discourse, climate, fiat, directive, felt pressure, or belief system, among other things. King Lear's oldest daughters, as *forces*, work in support of him in the first scene and work against him thereafter, but their *motivations* remain the same. Both things need to be taken into account in a productive script analysis.

2. STYLE

Script analysis leads to almost everything else that follows, but it leads most directly to a decision about the style of your production, and style has everything to do with your decisions about what the production is to be about, what you would like it to do, and what its primary modes of communication are.

The predominant styles of theatrical production in the English-speaking world are *naturalism* and *realism*.

> *Naturalism* emerges from nineteenth-century science and it has to do with understanding (or trying to understand) the laws of nature, including human nature. The basic drive of naturalism is cause and effect, so naturalistic theatre traces a logical, if manufactured, cause-and-effect throughline from a show's initiating action to its conclusion, each action clearly motivated by some prior action or condition (or character trait), and each leading with seeming inevitability to the next.
>
> Naturalism relies for its effect on its iconicity, for the resemblance between what's on stage and what the audience would recognize as its "real-life" equivalent. If you decide that your production will

be naturalistic, all of your choices will be made with a view to maintaining this resemblance and avoiding anything that could shatter the illusion.

Naturalism can, however, and often is, heightened in various ways so that events that could happen in the real world (and therefore do not shatter the illusion) come to take on resonance, significance, or symbolism that exceeds in lyrical or poetic ways the demands of the form. This is often called *poetic naturalism*.

Realism also relies on iconicity for its effects, but unlike naturalism its focus is not on cause and effect but on the unvarnished, unromantic representation of life and the world "as it is," with all its blemishes intact. It tells you a lot about realism to remember that the word is most often used in conjunction with adjectives such as "brutal" or "photographic."

Realism does not paint rosy pictures, and a director choosing this style not only has to avoid shattering the illusion, but also has to avoid anything decorative or sentimental.

Realism also has it variations, most prominently *hyperrealism* and *magic realism*. *Hyperrealism* creates a false, more detailed, and more clearly defined version of reality than realism itself, often de- or re-contextualized or placed in unusual circumstances, creating a simulation, or false reality. *Magic realism* uses an essentially realistic style or setting but incorporates events that are impossible in quotidian reality, often without commenting on the fact.

Naturalism and realism are usually understood in op-
position to *stylization*. There are an infinite number of ways
beyond poetic naturalism, hyperrealism, or magic realism in
which a production can be stylized. Most of them have to do
with an attempt to delve more deeply than the "mere" repro-
duction of life and the world in all of its messy and quotidian
detail in search of an essence of some kind. Most aim for
"truth" rather than settling for realism's facts or naturalism's
often limiting causalities. Although types of stylization are potentially infinite, I list some of the more familiar ones below
and attempt to give a sense of what uses they might serve.

Symbolism emerged in the late nineteenth century as
an idealist reaction to naturalism. It tends to focus on
the realm of the imagination, on dreams, and on spir-
ituality, and it attempts to approach truths through
a kind of indirection, endowing objects and images
with larger-than-life symbolic meaning. Symbolist
theatre often moves toward ritual in an attempt to
approach what it considers to be the deep and hidden
or intuitive truths of existence. It tends to operate in
broad, primarily visual strokes rather than in sub-
tleties and to employ an acting style that gestures
toward the ritualistic.

Impressionism has to do with perceptions and with
what mental impressions the world makes on individ-
uals. It is less concerned with depths than surfaces and
less concerned with root causes than with relations.
Its main concerns are the creation of atmosphere and

mood rather than deeply felt emotions and it requires a light directorial touch.

As its name implies, *expressionism* is generally concerned with the expression of emotion rather than the depiction of surface realities. It tends to be interested in individual psyches and mental states, often anguished ones. It relies for its effects on exaggeration and distortion and is dominated by sharp angles, bold or brooding colours, and an acting style that relies on gesture, mask, lyrical movement, and vocal expression—a style that naturalism would consider to be overwrought.

Surrealism is primarily interested in the unconscious and tends to work through the kinds of surprising juxtapositions and non sequiturs that are most familiar from dreams. In theatre it often involves the mythological, archetypal, and allegorical, and its primary languages are image and movement rather than the spoken word.

Minimalism involves the distillation of everything to its essentials, avoiding anything that is decorative or merely theatrical and employing a minimum of props, furnishings, or set pieces. It tends to be interested in the unspoken or unspeakable and even its use of language is most often sparse.

The *theatre of the absurd* is associated with a body of modernist drama by Beckett, Ionesco, Edward Albee, and others, but it can also be thought of as a style of staging. It is often (though not always) associated with an existentialist vision of existence without or preceding meaning, or of a world that operates by inscrutable and illogical forces. As its name suggests, it employs situations and conventions that are fundamentally absurd, if often eerily recognizable. In terms of staging, it often uses confined spaces, parodic gestures, and repetitive actions.

Epic theatre is the style invented and advocated by Bertolt Brecht. Epic theatre avoids immersion in the dramatic illusion and adopts a presentational style that operates by showing. This means an acting style in which actors "present" rather than attempt to merge with their characters and it involves, in acting and design, the selection of only those elements of people and the world that are relevant to understanding the social significance of the action. It's most useful for work that is explicitly political, because it attempts to portray action not as inevitable but as a function of human choice.

There are various types of *clowning*, but most involve an assumption of innocence on the part of sympathetic but naive characters-as-clowns that reveals in the world and worldliness that they try to negotiate a certain illogical decadence or corruption—a *loss* of innocence. Clowning usually involves physical comedy and requires actors with training in clown techniques.

Postmodernism, *poststructuralism*, and the *postdramatic* are related and overlapping styles (if indeed they *are* styles in the traditional sense) that can in practice be indistinguishable from one another and that often (though not always) aspire to be non-representational, focusing on affect and impact rather than character, story, or indeed even meaning.

Postmodernism emerged as a reaction to high modernist formalism with its enclosed structures of self-containment and self-referentiality. Most postmodern productions highlight uncertainty, employ structural openness, and tend toward interrogative rather than declarative modes.

Poststructuralism has as its central feature skepticism about all forms of certainty, unity, and totality, and a distrust of overarching or "master" narratives. It is deeply invested in explorations of form and it tends to mix styles and historical periods, deliberately placing them in contrast to one another.

Postdramatic performance is a more precise term than the other "posts," and is distinguished by a number of specific features: it disrupts familiar types of theatrical representation (including plot and character); it fractures temporal progression; it refuses to depict an enclosed fictional "world of the play"; it focuses on the materiality and independence of "text" (broadly understood); it employs digital and other media and intermediality; and it often employs a thick layering of intertextuality.

All three "posts" tend toward pastiche, paradox, irony, fragmentation, and the selective appropriation of other styles; all tend to employ metatheatricality; all presume a high level of audience sophistication; and all work to both denaturalize and defamiliarize everything they touch.

Performance style is closely related to form and genre, though style, form, and genre need not coincide or be mutually reinforcing. Some of the above styles are generally understood to be appropriate for tragedy, some for comedy, some for satire, some for farce, but productions that work against these common-sense pairings can be productive and powerful: expressionist farce can claim peculiar significance, for example, in mocking an overwrought world, and tragedy performed by clowns can be uniquely compelling and generate surprising new meanings while refusing to take itself too seriously.

Beyond the dominant western tradition there is a myriad of other styles, forms, and genres not considered above that range from Noh through Kabuki to Kutiyattam and Kathakali; from Japanese Bunraku through Islamic to Malaysian shadow and Vietnamese water puppetry; from Kunqu to Jingju (Chinese) Opera; and finally to innumerable ritual, ceremonial, and dance forms from Indigenous and other communities around the world. Many of these forms have been raided, distorted, appropriated, or treated *as* "mere styles" by western interculturalist directors, but most have their own rigidly coded communication systems, and few are available in any ethical way to theatre artists without membership in the specific cultures or communities and/or a lifetime of specialized training.

Many contemporary theatre artists, however, especially those impacted by the historical and contemporary effects of dominant or colonizing representational technologies on their lives and bodies, are constantly forging new styles to serve new purposes. Djanet Sears calls her *Harlem Duet* in performance a "rhapsodic blues tragedy," for example, and d'bi.young anitafrika refers to all of her stage work, which is grounded in the formal principles of Caribbean dub poetry, as "biomyth monodrama."

The selection (or invention) of a production's style is not a mechanical question of choosing your "ism," nor, indeed, are the styles I've listed (and the many others I haven't) entirely pure and distinct from one another. Nevertheless, an acute awareness of how style relates to function—to what you want to *do*—is essential for a director, and decisions about style precede all other decisions because they determine what skills will be required of the actors, designers, and other people involved.

3. PLANNING THE PROCESS

A rehearsal process is not a one-size-fits-all proposition, nor is it something that can be played by ear. Although directors tend to develop their own ways of working, each process is different, depending on the project. Designing and planning a process can't be left to chance, but needs to be a matter of translating analysis into procedure.

The key portions of your script analysis that are relevant to scheduling a rehearsal process that's appropriate to what you want to do are: determining your primary modes of communication, analyzing the characters or roles to be played by the actors, understanding the structure of the piece, and deciding on an appropriate style. Depending on what your analyses reveal in each of these areas, you'll have to put together a process that focuses on or prioritizes some kinds of work over others, and that determines the order in which you do things.

Posting Auditions

The first concern is preparing for auditions. Although some directors develop and work with a relatively consistent company of actors with whom they're familiar, most will also, with more or less frequency, be involved in auditioning, either through open calls or by invitation.

The theatre's administration or stage management will post an audition call, but should do so under your direction. The purpose of posting audition notices is to let actors decide whether to audition and, if they decide to do so, what's required of them.

1. You should begin by posting the requirements of the show; that is, you should post the *roles* that need to be filled by age, gender, and any other specific requirements. Don't indicate what the age, gender, etc. of the *actors* should be. They can decide what range they have and what roles they'd like to be considered for. Do make it clear at this stage if the production (or audition) involves particular personal exposure (such as nudity) or risk.

2. Secondly you should post what they're being asked to prepare: A contemporary monologue? A piece in verse? A comic monologue? A classical soliloquy? A sonnet? Some combination of these? Will they be expected to learn "sides" (portions of the script) in advance? They should also be told how long their

prepared piece(s) should be. Short, two- to three-min-
ute prepared pieces are usually long enough.

Finally, they should be told if you expect them to
prepare a movement piece or whether they will be
asked to sing, improvise, or do group work. What
you ask them to prepare will depend on the nature
of the script or project you're directing and should
emerge from your script analysis.

3. Actors should be told how long the entire audition will be and in a general sense what to expect. If
you're scheduling fifteen-minute auditions and asking
for two-minute prepared monologues, for example,
you should indicate what they might be asked to do
in the other thirteen minutes.

4. They should be asked to bring a resumé if they
haven't already submitted one. Auditions should be
scheduled with enough time to welcome and introduce actors and to work with them, enough space for
contemplation and note-taking, and in such a way as
to avoid fatigue.

You should also plan to schedule callbacks should you
need them, including the possibility of group callbacks
and group work, particularly if you are casting an ensemble project. For more on auditions and callbacks, consult
Section Five.

Scheduling the Process

With the help of stage management you'll need to draw up a provisional rehearsal and production schedule (always subject to change) that takes into account your approach and your needs, including coordination of rehearsal and production. When considering the following list, consult with subsequent sections to become familiar with what the implications and stakes are for each decision, and how each of your decisions relates to the requirements of your project.

1. *First meeting*: How long should it be? Who should be there? Who should present? Why?

2. *Design*: When and how will design be integrated into the process? Why? Consider sets, costumes, light, sound, and stylized movement.

3. *Floor plan*: When do you want the floor plan taped out in the rehearsal hall?

4. *Table work*: Do you want to allot time for group table work and analysis early in the production, or do you want to get people on their feet right away? Why?

5. *Physical and vocal warm-ups*: If you want to schedule these as part of the process, when, and for how long? Individual or group? Why?

6. Do you want to do *character work* prior to scene work or other aspects of the process? Why? Individual or group character work? Why? What *kind* of character work? Why?

7. *Calls*: Do you want all of the actors called to every rehearsal in order to build a sense of ensemble? Or will character and scene rehearsals be kept separate from one another in order to avoid actors' inappropriately picking up on one another's rhythms? If so, how long will they remain separate?

8. *Rehearsal sequencing*: Using your structure/unit breakdown from your script analysis, how will you rehearse the units in relation to one another? Sequentially? By actor/character grouping? Thematically? Why?

Sometimes it's useful to keep different plot strands and character groupings separate for as long as possible to allow them to develop their own momentum; at other times, when plot strands parallel and comment on one another, they are best rehearsed in parallel in order to highlight comparisons and contrasts.

Sometimes it's useful to rehearse the end of a show first, or early on, so that everyone knows where they're going; at other times the final scenes are best left untouched until the last minute in order to free up explorations that might best remain open-ended for as long as possible.

9. *Physical work*: Do you want to devote specific rehearsal time to such things as finding the characters' bodies, to developing movement vocabularies, or to doing physical exercises? Does the project require a movement coach or designer, choreographer, or fight coach? If so, how and when will their work be incorporated into the process?

10. *Blocking*: When and how do you plan to block the show? In advance with modifications in rehearsal? As an organic part of the rehearsal process? When will it be fixed, if ever?

11. *Transitions*: It's essential to decide on a style for transitions and to schedule time to rehearse them. When and how do you want to do this? Is this mostly to be done in rehearsal, with actors, or is it a matter for tech, to be done with stagehands and timed/coordinated with music and lights?

12. *Lines*: When do you want the actors to be off book (i.e., to have memorized their lines)?

13. *Prompts*: How do you want stage management to prompt and to correct errors? (Usually they will prompt only when an actor calls for a line and will correct persistent errors at the end of rehearsals.)

14. How much time will be devoted to *scene work* and when? How flexible will you be around

problem-solving and how much time should be scheduled for work "to be announced" (TBA)?

15. Do you need to schedule time for shooting *video* or *film* sequences involving actors? Do you need to schedule tech and editing time for this?

16. When will you need *rehearsal props and costumes*? When will you need final props and costumes? You will need an approximation early in rehearsals of any props or costumes such as hoop skirts, high heels, corsets, or canes that might have an impact on the actors' physicality.

17. When do you need to be *on set*?

18. *Tech*: When will you incorporate light and sound? How much time will be devoted to such things as level set, cue to cue, technical and dress runs? When? Why?

19. *Previews*: How many preview performances will you have (if any) and how will rehearsals and notes be scheduled between them?

All of these decisions need to be thought through carefully and justified in relation to your script analysis and to the considerations outlined in subsequent sections.

4. TALKING WITH DESIGNERS

Discussions with designers should normally take place well before casting, and in many cases should take place before script or project selection. In the best circumstances, designers are involved in the initial conceptualization of the show and continue to be involved throughout.

It can be useful to talk with designers conceptually, but it's often the case that a discussion with set, costume, prop, lighting, movement designers (see Section Ten), or scenographers will be best served by developing an imagistic rather than simply a conceptual vocabulary, while talking with sound designers will benefit from thinking in rhythms, tones, and pitches—though images and metaphors also work well.

It's best *not* to think in terms of actual design decisions—don't, that is, design the show yourself and ask designers simply to carry out your instructions or realize your vision. In the initial stages, at least, you should avoid even thinking in any detail about what you want the show on stage to look or sound like. Begin with much more associative thinking. But first:

1. Become thoroughly familiar with the location, normal use, size, shape, and amenities of your venue, with your playing space, and with the audience-stage

configurations and relationships available to you (see Section Nine). These determine to a considerable degree both who your audience is and how it's possible to use the space.

2. Make sure you know what your budget is, what workshop and building spaces can be utilized, and what technical personnel are available to you. These things can frame your decisions about the structures and materials you can use.

3. Review your script analysis, paying particular attention to your summaries of what the show is about, its primary modes of communication, its structure, and its rhythms. Also review your decisions about the production's style.

For later discussions with set designers you'll also need to have analyzed the script from the point of view of entrances, exits, and the flow of the action so that they'll be able to develop a floor plan that suits your needs. For both set and costume designers in particular you'll need to talk through your character analyses and their own so that they know who will be living in their spaces and wearing their clothes. For everyone, think early and often about transitions—these affect the set, costume changes, and especially light and sound—because they can have a huge impact on the shape and rhythm of the show.

4. At the first design meetings try to develop meta-phoric and imagistic ways of communicating what you imagine to be the show's mood and character. It almost always helps to bring some things to design meetings to illustrate in visual and tactile ways how you're thinking about the show's imagery, texture, palette, taste, shape, and spatiality: its feel. Paintings and photographs are good sources, but so might be fabrics, materials, patterns, objects, sculptures, pieces of music, films, video clips, poems, stories, newspaper articles, games, food, or drink.

Don't be too literal. Try in the early stages to avoid indicating what you want; instead try to illustrate how the show feels to you and what it's about. Metaphorical thinking also works well with sound and movement designers. This allows all of the designers the scope to invent and to participate in full partnership, and the result is always better than either you or they would have achieved independently. One of the best initial design presentations I've seen involved a student director indicating the feel of a show by Norm Foster set in summer in Muskoka's cottage country by dropping a pair of wet jeans onto a wooden floor, evoking with considerable precision the texture and acoustic qualities required. Another, trying to communicate the feel of a stage direction in Judith Thompson's *White Biting Dog* that read "sound of a skateboard," said she wanted it to feel like the sound of the soul leaving the body.

Good designers will have done their own analysis and preparation, and it's essential that you listen to these closely—they'll almost always reveal things that you've missed. And designers will also in most cases bring materials with them—sketches, books, videos, music—that reflect their thinking. The combination of your stuff and their stuff can be quite exciting as a starting point.

5. Meet early and often, sharing ideas and moving gradually toward something more specific. Adjust to how the designers you work with like to communicate and prefer to work. Some will themselves bring materials with them to show you what they're thinking, some will sketch or paint on the spot as you discuss things, some prefer to improvise in three dimensions with maquettes, and some will work conceptually.

In all cases they're looking for a response from you. Be prepared to tell them what parts of what they present excite you or feel right to you and what parts don't, or that you don't understand. Ask for clarifications, expansions. Once you're sure you understand, suggest modifications, combinations, or different approaches. Don't reject things too readily, but don't hesitate to say no to ideas or suggestions that you know don't work with what you're imagining.

6. Once you're at the stage of set designers presenting actual renderings of proposed designs, think these through carefully, and "walk" the designs through the show (with set models and proportional figures you can do this quite literally). This might involve thinking through the blocking that a floor plan facilitates (or doesn't), the patterns and rhythms of movement it imposes, the entrances and exits it makes available, and the general ways in which it shapes the space, both vertically and horizontally.

This might also involve thinking through relationships between characters and how these are reflected in proposed costume designs, as it might involve thinking through whether and how costumes might restrict or enable movement and gesture (you don't want someone who has to do somersaults wearing a hoop skirt—and the designers may not know you have somersaults in mind).

In every case ask questions before raising objections. Chances are the answers will satisfy you or even expand your ways of thinking about what you can do.

7. As soon as you begin to move beyond the metaphorical stage to potential realizations, involve or consult production management to make sure that what you're imagining together is possible and manageable within the constraints of budget, workshop time, and personnel. Production managers have been known to veto onstage waterfalls.

8. Continue to consult and communicate with designers throughout the rehearsal process as new discoveries occur that effect their work and along with it the feel and evolution of the show. The more designers can be present and involved in rehearsals—particularly lighting, sound, and movement designers—the better.

5. AUDITIONING AND CASTING

Whether or not you hold auditions, casting, for most productions, is the most crucial phase in mounting a production. The casting decisions you make will frame almost all other decisions about the show and will do more than anything else to determine its character and quality. Casting determines what bodies, voices, and personalities will inhabit the roles that most immediately represent the production to your audience. Once a show is cast, many subsequent decisions circulate around those actors.

Auditions

If you're holding auditions, make sure you're prepared. Know the roles that you're casting for well—your script analysis is crucial here—and know what you're looking for in each role. But be prepared to be surprised. Actors in auditions will sometimes show you something in a character or role that changes your way of thinking, and it's important to be open to this.

Try to make the auditions pleasant for everyone involved and keep the tone upbeat and professional.

1. Prepare the room. Make sure you have any props and furniture (chairs, tables, etc.) available that you might want to use during the auditions, and make sure you have water available (nervous actors' mouths tend to get dry).

2. Make sure that there's a stage manager, assistant director, or other member of the company in the room during auditions. Try to have gender balance among those present, and where there are cultural, sexual, or other sensitivities at play make sure these are accounted for: it's not appropriate or productive, for example, for a young queer woman of colour to audition before a room of older straight white men.

3. Begin by doing what you can to establish a professional atmosphere and to make the actors feel welcome. Introduce yourself and others in the room by name and role in the production. Chat a bit at the beginning about what you see on the actors' resumés, previous experience they've had, skills they list, and other roles they've played (unless they seem to be uncomfortable chatting and just want to get down to work, in which case go with that).

Invite them to provide whatever introduction to their audition piece they want to give in order to contextualize or explain the circumstances and then invite them to begin whenever they're ready. Show everyone respect: they have gone to considerable trouble to prepare and be there and are doing you a favour by auditioning.

4. Allow all actors to go through their prepared pieces in full and without interruption (if they stick to their allotted time), even if you know immediately that you don't want to cast them. Allow them to restart if they need to.

Sometimes it's the actors who are most nervous, or most sensitive to disruptions or distractions in the room, who end up being most nuanced in rehearsal and performance.

5. Make notes, preferably immediately after each audition. If you make notes during auditions, do so discreetly without taking your attention away from the actors auditioning. It can throw actors to have no one apparently paying attention to them.

6. Try to see potential cast members in relation to one another and include potential pairings or groupings in your notes as you go along.

7. If you have any glimmer of interest in particular actors, work with them. There are actors who are brilliant in their prepared pieces but with whom you won't be able to work, and there are actors whose prepared pieces are ordinary but who respond well to direction. Some actors will respond well to your

particular style of directing; some, however strong they seem otherwise, won't work well with you, or won't understand what you're asking them to do.

Ask actors you are potentially interested in to do their audition pieces again, but ask them to change the given circumstances or to change the address (who they're speaking to), making specific suggestions. Give them a particular or different task to do while they're doing the piece, give them a new motive, or increase the stakes. Avoid asking them to play attitudes or emotions and avoid offering anything that sounds like criticism.

The purpose of working with actors in these ways is to find out how flexible they are, and how responsive they are to your style of direction. This is usually much more important than how well they perform a prepared piece.

8. If it's useful to you, find out what other skills they may have (singing, dancing, juggling, mime, clown, etc.).

9. If you need to find out how well they improvise, or gauge their movement skills, give them an exercise that shows this.

Improvs can be designed either around the actor's prepared audition piece or around something to do with the role you have in mind for them.

Movement exercises are most usefully designed around testing spontaneous physical responses from a position of readiness (a relaxed stance with legs apart at hip width and knees slightly bent, poised lightly on the balls of the feet).

Be encouraging. These impromptu tasks can be daunting when performed in front of strangers in the context of an audition.

10. If it isn't already apparent, find out how well they project their voices. Do some vocal work with them if necessary, especially if you'll be working in a space that's larger or less acoustically resonant than the hall in which you're holding auditions (or in which they're used to performing). Size matters. Actors who are powerful and effective in the intimate confines of the Aki Studio may not have the chops for the Festival stage at Stratford; actors who blow you away at the nine-hundred-seat Theatre Hall at the National Arts Centre may seem overblown at a Fringe venue in Edmonton.

11. If you have specific roles in mind for individual actors, you may want to ask them to do cold readings from the script (having selected passages for each character in advance). If it's helpful, ask your stage manager or assistant director to read with them.

Don't expect too much from this exercise. Not all good actors do cold readings well, and many come into their own only once they've done some preparation. Cold readings *can*, however, allow you to hear actors' voices in character and can give you a sense of their initial, instinctive responses to particular roles and ways of speaking.

12. At the end of each audition thank the actor and indicate when and how she'll be notified about either callbacks or casting.

Callbacks

Callbacks are not routine and are often extra trouble for everyone, so don't have them if you don't need to, and if you do have them, be clear about exactly what new information you're trying to find out. There are a few guidelines you can follow:

1. Only call back people who have a good chance of being cast.

2. Design callbacks to find out the specific things you need to know, not just to give people a second chance or to ask them to do the same things again.

3. If appropriate or useful, call people back in pairs, character groupings, or full ensembles to discover chemistry (or lack of it) between actors, to find out about how well they work together, or how well they might work as part of an ensemble. Pair or group them carefully as potential casts in order to find out what you want to know.

Informing About Results

Make sure that everyone who auditioned is informed of the result as soon as possible with professionalism and respect. Everyone should be thanked for auditioning.

Casting

Whether you're holding auditions or working with known quantities, cast carefully. The following is a list of things to take into consideration.

1. Be mindful of combinations and chemistries between actors. A perfect Romeo may not be perfect for the Juliet you have in mind.

2. Try not to cast to physical type or past experience. Actors are always best in roles that stretch and challenge them, but not *far* beyond the limits of their current abilities or experience.

3. Cast actors with whom you feel you can work, those who have responded well to your directions in the past or in their auditions. Avoid those who can only do well what they've prepared to do, who play themselves, or who appear to be the same character in whatever roles they're cast.

4. Be aware that the flashiest actor in auditions is rarely the best one, unless the role calls for a specific kind of flashiness. Cast actors in whom you find some depth and actorly intelligence and in whom you can see the potential to grow.

Once casting is complete, make sure that stage management provides those cast with copies of the script and as much information as possible about the scheduling and location of rehearsals. You may want to invite those cast to be in touch with you prior to the beginning of the rehearsal period with any questions or concerns they have. Such questions and concerns sometimes surface only after they've read the script with their own roles in mind.

6. FIRST MEETING

The first meeting of the company will have been considered as part of your rehearsal plan from the outset, and how you conduct it sets the stage for the rest of the rehearsal process.

There are some essential elements to this meeting, but the rest are up to you and dependent upon the specifics of your project. The meeting should involve as much of the company as possible, but definitely assistant directors, stage management, designers, and actors. Theatre administration is usually also invited to all or part of the meeting, including the producer, publicist, artistic director, general manager, and especially the production manager and technical director, though sometimes they only attend for the read-through, if there is one.

The process should start with *introductions* in as comfortable a way as possible—usually oiled by some kind of treats or refreshments (non-alcoholic). It'll be necessary after that to do some *organizational business*, and this is best left to stage management: getting contracts signed, electing an equity deputy if the show is being performed under an Actors' Equity agreement, getting contact information from the company, and setting out procedural guidelines for the process (the posting of rehearsal calls and notes, procedures for the running of rehearsals, and so on).

Stage management will also usually talk about rehearsal protocols, but you may want to address the company as well about any special protocols you want to see observed in the rehearsal hall or beyond, including who is or is not invited to attend or participate in rehearsals, what kind of participation or discussion is or is not welcome, the treatment of the space, and behaviour and communication outside of rehearsals.

Some directors believe strongly in the sacredness of the rehearsal space and don't allow food, newspapers, phones, tablets, or other distractions into the room, where all attention must be focused on the work at hand. Others feel that the rehearsal hall should be a comfortable living space where the actors can relax into their work with all of their familiar comforts at hand.

Some directors believe strongly in the privacy of rehearsals, feeling that everything that happens in rehearsal stays in rehearsal, and that this frees the actors to follow their impulses without fear of repercussions. Others believe that the more public the process is the more the community will be involved and the more useful feedback the company will receive.

It's important for you to carve out your position on these things and to clarify and explain it at the outset in order to avoid misunderstandings later. But try to get the business/discipline end of things out of the way before you turn to the creative parts of the meeting.

You'll often see the first meeting referred to as the "first read-through," and that can be a central feature, but this is only the case if there is a script and if you decide that this is the best way to proceed.

If the show is not heavily text driven, if it's an ensemble piece, or if it's otherwise appropriate, you may prefer to begin with group exercises. If so, physical and perhaps vocal warm-ups should be part of this—often best led by members of the company, and always appropriate to the show you're doing.

You may choose to build the ensemble by doing such things as name and trust exercises (but see Section Eleven, below), you may wish to do improvisations around specific scenarios or themes that explore the actors' relationships to some central elements in the show, or you may develop show-specific games or exercises that work for you.

If you do begin with a read-through it's a good idea to sit in a circle in which everyone can see and make eye contact with one another. Everyone from this point forward should have a copy of the script, a pencil, and an eraser with them at all times (stage management will have seen to this). Don't ask for or expect "acting" in a first read-through and try to make sure that the read-through isn't competitive—that actors aren't showing off. But do ask them to lift the scenes off the page by making eye contact with the actor(s) they're addressing and do ask them to listen very closely to one another.

It's important at this stage for everyone to feel they can stop and ask questions about the meaning or pronunciation of words, or about unfamiliar concepts. You need to be prepared to answer any questions that come up, and if you can't, say so, promising to find out for the next meeting. Everyone should take a note of these for future reference. You can't have family members pronouncing their last names differently, unless of course that's an issue in a play about a dysfunctional family.

You should watch and listen for relationships developing among the actor/characters during the read-through: listen to the ways the voices work together or against one another, the actors' rhythms, and the chemistry among them. It's usually best not to follow along in the script, which you should already know inside out and backwards; rather you should watch and listen closely to how the company is beginning to work together.

Once the reading is complete you may want to talk about why you chose this particular show, why it matters to you, what it has to do with the world and the community at this particular place and time, why you think they should care about it. Tell them as much as you can about what you know at this point. This may involve bringing in research—books, pictures, film clips, music, etc.—which may be displayed and made available throughout the rehearsal process.

You may also want to invite members of the company to talk about what they care about in the script, what interests them, and what it connects with for them. And you may want to invite them to bring their own research to the rehearsal hall to share with other members of the company as the process evolves. These talks and this research are crucial because they create common understandings on which everything else builds.

Sometimes you'll see the director's presentation referred to as a "concept" talk ("here's my idea for the show"), and in some circumstances it can be that, but it doesn't have to be. I prefer to think of it as providing a con*text* within which rehearsal explorations will take place—and a context doesn't have to be merely ideas or concepts. Often it will be a painting, or a film, or a poem, or a piece of music that the company will keep returning to for inspiration.

You may or may not want or be able to invite your designers to do a "show and tell" at this meeting, displaying a maquette, floor plan and elevations, and costume renderings. In some cases and in some ideal worlds these can actually evolve along with rehearsals (as can lighting and sound design), but this is a rare luxury.

If the designs are in fact complete by the first meeting, it's a good idea to do a show and tell so that the company, again, knows the context within which they're working—knows the costumes they'll be wearing and the space(s) they'll be moving through. Ask the designers to present their designs themselves and invite the company to ask questions.

Depending on the show and the rehearsal schedule, you may want to jump right in to the first steps in the rest of your process—beginning with whatever you feel is most appropriate (table work, shared script analysis, physical exercises—whatever). But it's usually best to take a substantial break after the first meeting before moving into the next phases of the process, if you can. This could mean breaking for the day, taking a lunch break, or just taking fifteen minutes for coffee, but it should be clear that you are shifting to a different register, and ideally there should be enough break time at this point for folks to digest what they've heard and seen in the first encounter.

Whether it's within the first meeting or in subsequent table work, it's essential, before moving on to character and scene work, that all the major given circumstances (times, dates, places, relationships) be established if they're not already clear from the script—and in the case of Shakespeare and his contemporaries as well as in many contemporary plays, they aren't. These are ultimately directorial decisions.

7. PRODUCTION NOTES, PRODUCTION MEETINGS, AND FITTINGS

Production Notes

Once rehearsals begin, you'll receive daily copies of production notes from stage management. These are circulated to all departments (sets, costumes, props, lights, sound, publicity, production management, and administration) and are intended to provide daily updates on requirements that have emerged from rehearsal, as props are added or cut, the need for pockets, hooks, Velcro or quick changes emerges, or anything else evolves that might have an impact on design and tech. Departments may respond to these notes with questions, comments, and updates on their progress.

You should read these notes carefully to make sure that they accurately reflect what you want, weigh in on the conversation (only) where necessary, or better, talk to stage management about any discrepancies.

Production Meetings

In addition to notes, there will be regular production meetings, usually once a week, usually called and chaired by the production manager, and involving representatives from all departments. Each department will report in turn, and some will have questions for you. Sometimes you'll know the answers immediately, sometimes not. When you don't know yet, say so, and try to give a sense of when you will. Always welcome thoughts and suggestions, but neither feel pressured into answering before you're ready nor delay answering unnecessarily. Brilliant ideas and suggestions can emerge from any quarter in a production meeting, and you need to be open to them.

Some of the issues that emerge at production meetings may have to do with budget. If budget constraints are tight (they usually are), you may find yourself having to decide where and what to cut, and when to divert funds from one department to another. Alternately, it may be possible to use cheaper materials or equipment. It's crucial that you listen carefully to the discussion, weigh the options, and make clear where your priorities lie. If you can save an important costume by doing away with running water, if a painted flat can replace a costly set piece with no significant loss, or if doing away with costly wigs can save the rest of the show, you may have to make these choices.

One of the departments at a production meeting is publicity. Publicists are rarely in rehearsal and may or may not have read a script, but their job is to represent the show accurately (and positively) to your potential audience based on what the producer or producing company tells them. It's important, in light of this, to maintain control of the show's representation. You should make sure that you exercise your right of approval and refusal of press releases, publicity photos, and any representations of the show in posters, programs, or on social media. (This right should be articulated in your contract.) Your show should be made to look good, compelling, interesting, and entertaining, but it should also be represented accurately in order to avoid ultimately disappointing audience expectations.

You will probably also be asked to take active part in producing publicity materials for social media. Increasingly directors are asked to direct filmic-style "trailers" (usually YouTube videos), to tweet or post on Facebook or other social media about the rehearsal process, to write blogs or journal entries, or even to take and post photos documenting the ongoing process. It's important to be willing to participate; it's also important not to let this take over, or take up too much time and energy.

Fittings

Stage management, in tandem with rehearsals and in consultation with the wardrobe department, will be scheduling fittings for the cast. It's important that you let stage management know that you want to be invited, and it's essential that, apart from initial measurement sessions, you attend. Part of the reason for this, of course, is to make sure that the costumes do the work that you want them to as responsibility moves from designers to wardrobe and from design to application (that is, from design sketches and fabric samples of which you've approved, to the actual finding and building of costumes). Discussions with designers and wardrobe about cut, fit, materials, and detail during fittings can often pre-empt problems later.

The other reason for attending fittings, however, is to be there for your actors, to make sure that they feel safe and comfortable and that they'll be able to do what they need to do in the costume that's been found or is being made for them. Designers and technicians may or may not have heard that an actor will be doing cartwheels while wearing that skirt, or that the silk shirt they've selected will be drenched in blood nightly.

Finally, it's important that the materials being used or chosen not only have the right look, from an audience's point of view, but also feed the actor's imagination and physicality in supportive and appropriate ways. This extends from the difference in feel between, say, silk, satin, polyester, cotton, denim, or wool, to choices made about unseen items of clothing. Men feel and behave differently in boxer shorts than in briefs, a sports bra has a very different feel from a support bra, a lace bra, or no bra at all, and there are certain things that a corset does to an actor's body that can be either useful or disastrous. Similar considerations have to be given to footwear, from flip-flops to sneakers to heels or boots, which have an impact on a show that extends far beyond what the audience sees. And hats, of course, have to work with lights.

8. CHARACTER, ROLE, AND TASK

At this point the ordering of the process begins to vary considerably depending on the project and the process planning you've done. Some directors on some projects will begin with table work, some with physical work finding characters' bodies, some with improvisations and explorations, some with various kinds of scene work. But at some point (and in some cases throughout the process) most will have to address the question of how the actors think about what they're doing.

In contemporary Canadian theatre what they're doing is usually "playing a character" (or, in the case of doubling, characters), but this is not always or necessarily the case, and even when it is, it doesn't always mean approaching the work in the same way.

"Character," as it's most often used today (to mean either the characteristics of an individual personality in the real world or a figure in fiction, theatre, or film), is largely an invention of the nineteenth century. Throughout much of the history of western theatre actors played "parts" or "roles" when they weren't playing themselves, and in many non-western traditions the western idea of playing a character is seen as a distinct, sometimes quaint style, and is by no means taken for granted.

"To act, to do, to perform": Character, Role, Task

Actors or performers are generally asked to do one or some combination of three things: acting characters, playing roles, or performing tasks.

1. *Acting* is something peculiar to theatre and film, and it is associated with certain training and disciplinary regimes (such as Stanislavski's System, the American Method, Butoh, and clown, plus various voice and movement methodologies).

2. *Performing* has different and broader resonances, and while it generally encompasses acting (we talk about actors' performances), it comprises many other things as well, and may not involve playing a role at all. It's the (usually unrealized) goal of much performance art, for example, simply to *do*, often as a one-off, avoiding mimesis, "being oneself," and establishing between performer and audience a kinesthetic relationship that attempts not to involve pretense (which is what, some would argue, distinguishes performance art from theatre).

But we also, significantly, talk about technological performance (high-performance motor oil), corporate performance (performance reviews), stock-market performance, and athletic performance, and most of these involve reliable repetition (the French word for rehearsal). Richard Schechner's definition of performance is "twice behaved behaviour," or "restored behaviour."

3. *Doing*—accomplishing a task—can be understood as an all-encompassing word including both acting and performing, but it doesn't necessarily involve either *mimesis* (imitation) or repetition. It obtains in all areas of animal and human life, and, as I've suggested above, is one of the things that performance art often aspires to.

But like acting and performing, doing something usually implies intentionality, and also has overtones of efficacy: acting, doing, and performance, that is, usually aspire to accomplish something, and this has to do with your original reason for staging your production.

Performing a Role

To perform a role is perhaps best understood as to pay attention to and imitate or indicate (point to) behaviour and action, without the need to explore psychological depth or motivation and without the need to merge performer with role. It is mimetic (in the sense that it involves Aristotle's "imitation of an action") and representational (in the sense that the audience recognizes what or whom the performance is intended to invoke), but the recognition it invites does not necessarily involve identification. Performing a role usually involves a degree of demonstration of behaviour and manner, and is a useful way of thinking about what actors do in satire or in social-action theatre.

Executing a Task

To do, or execute a task (or several tasks at once) in the theatre is simply to carry out some prescribed behaviour (sometimes while saying lines) without concern about motivation or effect. The theatre company best known for using this method is New York's Wooster Group, who try to avoid the identification of actor with character, or to avoid the actor's settling comfortably into a role, by assigning complex and often difficult tasks to their performers that often result in fascinating postmodern social performances or displays involving individual multiplicity and contradiction.

Audiences in such shows do not identify with either character or actor, but their imaginations are activated in piecing together performative fragments of behaviour. On the other hand, giving tasks can be useful even in naturalistic theatre to "take the pressure off the text"—to free the actor from overthinking.

Acting a Character

To act a character in most contemporary theatre in North America is to do one of two things:

1. Attempt to a greater or lesser degree to merge the actor with the character in such a way as to make them indistinguishable for audiences (this is the goal of most of the training offered—not always accurately—under the banner of Stanislavski's System or the

American Method as developed at Lee Strasberg's
Actors Studio in New York); or

2. Present selected characteristics of a character without such a merging, standing outside of the role and
commenting or inviting judgment on the choices
made by that character in its fictional historical and
social setting. This is the goal of Brecht's Epic theatre,
where the actor is doubly positioned both inside and
outside of the character she plays.

Acting a character usually begins with some kind of naturalism; that is, it begins with the assumption that behaviour
is the result of some cause or causes and issues in some effects
that then become the causes of subsequent actions. In Epic
theatre the causes are the result of historicized human choices
and they lead to (implicitly avoidable) effects. In naturalism
behaviour is understood to be the result of "human nature"
that is implicitly unchanging.

However problematic this last assumption may be, especially for those interested in social change, it's at the basis
of most current understandings of character in the theatre,
which assume that it's possible and desirable for actors to
"get inside" the characters they're playing, to understand
their motivations (or subtext), and imaginatively to position
themselves in the circumstances faced by the characters—to
identify with them—as a way of bringing those characters to
life and inviting audience identification (or empathy) as well.

Developing naturalistically based characters often involves probing actions and speeches for subtext, developing

backstory (what happened in their past that made them the way they are), and fleshing out such things as the characters' tastes and preferences that are not provided in the script (what kind of car do they drive, clothes do they wear, drink do they drink, food do they eat, and so on).

This type of exploration is not limited to strictly naturalistic theatre. Often various kinds of stylization begin from a naturalistic base in order to highlight certain aspects of the behaviour that's being performed or imitated.

Minimalism will often begin with naturalistic explorations before stripping away fussy naturalistic details to achieve greater clarity.

Expressionism will often probe character for deep-seated psychological motivations that are then played out in an exaggerated, larger-than-life manner to highlight a supposed psychological "truth" that exceeds realism's mere "facts."

Epic theatre will often select naturalistic details that have particular significance in explaining the social rather than psychological causes of character choices, or will present naturalistic scenarios before rupturing them with various alienation devices that eschew identification in favour of judgment.

Character, Role, and Task in Rehearsal

Once you've decided what it is you want your actors to do, you need to establish a process that supports their work. Much of what follows here and in the remainder of this book assumes that you're working, if only provisionally, with some variation on, extension, or critique of naturalism. This is partly because you'll find that naturalism is at the base of the training most of your actors will have received in the English-speaking world. It is also what will frame the expectations of most of your audiences.

There are various options concerning where to begin. You may want to start with table work and group analysis or plunge right in to physical or scene work, but the first steps in exploring character involve some combination of:

1. *Table work*: This involves exploring with individual actors or with the complete cast many of the things you'll have considered in your script analysis, including the show's given circumstances, what each of the characters says, what is said about them, what they do, and what the relationships among the characters are.

Table work also involves getting the story straight and making decisions about those circumstances that *aren't* given—developing backstories; character sketches; solidifying the place, time, and weather conditions for each scene; and identifying other contextual situations (is the action taking place during a revolution, a war, a jubilee, an election, an economic downturn?). It is important at this early stage to make sure that everyone is working from the same page.

If the play is in verse or other kinds of heightened language you'll need to work with actors who aren't experienced with this on how to speak the verse and how to read, understand, inhabit and play the author's characteristic language and style. If such instruction is beyond your competence or time commitment, you'll need to hire a voice or text coach.

Table work usually means going through the play line by line and scene by scene in order to make sure everyone shares the same answers to all the questions—and a rule of thumb that should be made explicit in this process is that there are no stupid questions. This is a point where your and others' research comes in handy, and it's worth having notes and resources with you in the rehearsal hall throughout.

Some actors are impatient with table work and are anxious to get on their feet; some revel in it because it's safe and postpones the risky business of committing themselves physically and emotionally to specific choices. As director you need to strike a balance between these impulses and intuit when the time for table work is over.

2. *Exploring the characters' voices*: This can take place either during table work or once the actors are on their feet, but it ultimately includes close, embodied analysis of the ways the characters speak, including their rhythms, syntax, diction, tricks of

speech, and imagery (as discussed above in Section One). The *way* a character speaks is usually more telling than what they say. Their diction (choice of words), figures of speech, and choice of images can often say a great deal about their background and experience, their speech rhythms and syntax (particularly as they vary) can say a lot about their state of mind.

3. *Finding the characters' bodies*: Once the actors have a good initial sense of their characters there are various exercises that can help them move from their own to their characters' bodies (see Section Eleven, below) and can provide them with a kind of physical shorthand into character.

Bodies are sculpted by personal histories, by the work one does for a living (a farmer does not move the way a tennis pro or a stockbroker does). They are shaped by the degree of confidence one has, and by a myriad of other forces that act upon them. Often the most direct route into character is in fact physical rather than psychological—discovering even through mimicry what it feels like emotionally to inhabit a particular body (this is the method that was used in Paul Thompson's collective creations at Toronto's Theatre Passe Muraille in the 1970s).

For productions in which movement is a primary mode of communication, particularly non-naturalistic productions, it's ideal to hire a movement coach or movement designer, as discussed in Section Ten.

4. *Scene work*: Before or after doing table or character work, before or after the show's floor plan has been taped in the rehearsal hall, with or without blocking the scenes, and with or without consciousness of such things as audience-stage relationships and sightlines, you'll have to get the actors on their feet working on scenes.

With a big cast it's often important to introduce some elements of blocking and some awareness of audience-stage relationships early on. If actors are continually negotiating the space and avoiding bumping into one another it's difficult for them to concentrate on their work.

With a smaller cast you may want to explore scenes with individual actors, in pairs, or in small groups, only concerning yourself with blocking and movement insofar as it expresses character and character relationships, and only when it is discovered by the actors themselves. Often this is a very effective way of exploring subtext and negotiating interpretations among the cast.

It's wise in scene work to begin with explorations, opening up possibilities, trying out various options, and making discoveries before moving on in later stages of the rehearsal process to make decisions (each of which narrows down the options for future choices).

There are two general rules of thumb for scene work from this point forward in most kinds of theatre that consider actors as creative collaborators rather than as simply servants of the director's individual vision: *never give line readings* (that is, never tell actors or demonstrate to them how to deliver a line) and *never give physical demonstrations* of how you want them to move.

Discussions and rehearsal work should generally be about *why* an actor is saying or doing something rather than about telling, showing, or discussing *how* to do it.

If a moment is working, it's best not even to ask why—delving into motivations and intentions is best reserved for problem-solving (when actors don't *know* why they are saying or doing something) or negotiating conflicting decisions (when the "whys" of two actors in a scene aren't working together or are working at cross purposes). These are discussed in Section Twelve.

The use of improvisation and games will also be discussed in Section Twelve, but apart from introductory and trust-building exercises it's usually not a good idea to start with them; they, too, are best reserved for problem-solving and they always work best with a particular purpose in mind.

9. SPACE, BLOCKING, AND PROXEMICS

You'll be working with space throughout your rehearsal process, from initial design meetings through blocking and staging transitions to final adjustments going into the run, and understanding how space works in the theatre is crucial to your role as director.

The first consideration, and one that shapes all others, is in most instances out of your control. This is the performance venue, including its location, neighbourhood, history, and the mandate and audience for its resident theatre company (if any), all of which can determine what kind of audience you might expect and therefore your show's "address" (both its location and who it's addressing).

Although some venues allow for a certain amount of flexibility, venue in most instances dictates the size of the audience and stage space, the relationship between them, and also, crucially, the configuration of the stage in relationship to the audience.

Audience-Stage Relationships

There are several basic types of audience-stage relationship that occur in a number of variations and combinations:

1. The *proscenium* (figure 1), the most familiar in western theatre and the closest in feel to television and cinema, in which the audience faces the stage frontally and there is some kind of architectural division between them—traditionally a proscenium arch framing the stage, from which may hang a curtain that lifts and descends to open and close the show, as well as between acts.

Curtains have been used with decreasing frequency in recent decades, but there usually remains something resembling a proscenium arch, a stage lip, and sometimes even a "raked" stage (sloping toward

Figure 1: Proscenium stage.

the audience). Almost always there is a space between the audience and the stage that ranges in size from a full orchestra pit to a gap of five or ten feet, and often the audience is also raked to slope upwards away from the stage. Upstage of the proscenium arch itself (sometimes even in front of it) there may or may not be wings and wing space, a crossover behind the stage, or a fly gallery above.

The proscenium emphasizes the division between the audience and the stage, frames the stage as a picture, positions the audience very much as spectators, voyeurs, or even consumers, and positions the show itself as "to-be-looked-at." The proscenium also tends to emphasize the represented action—the already complete story being told—over the "eventness," in the present, of the performance itself. Most other configurations try to work against this objectification

Figure 2: Thrust stage.

and distancing and can work to facilitate a greater sense of shared space and time.

2. A *thrust* configuration (figure 2) is one in which the stage, with or without a balcony area above, thrusts from one wall of the theatre (behind which there may or may not be backstage facilities) into an audience that surrounds it on three sides, usually raked away from the stage at a steep angle. Most thrust arrangements include *vomitoria*, (exits/entrances through or beneath the audience), often placed diagonally across from upstage entrances and exits. A thrust stage can function effectively as a platform for declamation and can easily configure the event as a kind of public forum for the negotiation of meaning and values.

Figure 3: Amphitheatre.

3. An *amphitheatre* (figure 3) can combine elements of a proscenium with elements of a thrust in that it usually has a circular or semicircular playing area (in Greek theatre the *orchestra*), arranged in front of a stage or stage building (in Greek theatre the *skene*), and extending into a semicircular or bowl-shaped audience (in Greek theatre the *theatron*). Because it often operates at a very large scale, usually outdoors but sometimes today in large stadiums, an amphitheatre tends to support spectacle and declamation over subtlety or intimacy.

4. A *traverse* (or alley, or corridor) stage (figure 4) bisects the audience, which is located on either side of it. The stage in this configuration can feel like a runway, with exits and entrances at either end. A traverse arrangement is difficult to block and to light, but can be useful for intimate, presentational, or metatheatrical shows.

Figure 4: Traverse stage.

5. In *theatre-in-the-round* (or sometimes in-the-square, rectangle, or even triangle or diamond) (figure 5) the audience surrounds the stage on all sides, usually raked away from it. Depending on the scale, theatre-in-the-round can be intimate and empowering for audiences, or, in the case of large-scale events such as Olympic openings, can effectively support certain kinds of spectacular or processional events.

6. *Promenade theatre* can involve any number of configurations simultaneously or successively, as audience and actors both move throughout a shared space or multiple spaces.

7. The *black box* (figure 6) is usually a small, flexible space that can employ more than one of the above configurations, but implies a certain intimacy between

Figure 5: Theatre-in-the-round.

the audience and the stage and a sense, at least, of shared space.

Any of these configurations may or may not involve the environmental or site-specific use of space, in which the space itself conveys significance rather than attempting to disappear as a neutral or empty vessel that is filled by the production. Each configuration can occur in various auditorium sizes and audience-stage proximities.

It's important to be fully conscious throughout the rehearsal process, particularly if you're working in a rehearsal hall that's configured differently from the performance space, of where the audience will be, how close they'll be to the performers, and what the nature of that relationship will be, not only because this affects sightlines and vocal, gestural, and movement size, but because it can determine what kinds

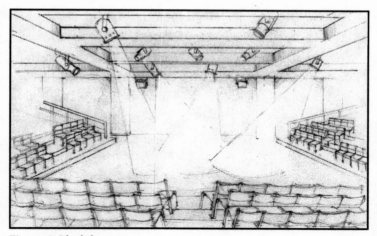

Figure 6: Black box.

of groupings are useful and effective, where powerful stage positions are, and how focus is achieved.

A thrust or in-the-round arrangement, for example, can often reward the use of clusters of actors facing outward from one another toward different portions of the audience (see figure 2), while a proscenium or amphitheatre usually demands some sort of frontal orientation, in which actors' backs face the audience only infrequently.

Traverse staging always plays against the stage's strong horizontal axis, movement along which can get tedious; theatre-in-the-round takes circular movements and geometrical angles as its baseline; and thrusts make considerable use of diagonals that bisect the stage, though these can be overdone and, again, become tedious.

Similar care has to be given to the analysis and use of (vertical) levels, which of course effect sightlines and inflect power relationships, and which also work differently in proscenium, thrust, traverse, and in-the-round configurations (not to mention their considerable power in promenade, environmental, site-specific, and other more variable arrangements).

And of course it's crucial to remember that these various configurations and contiguities can delimit the lighting options that are available. Three-point lighting, for example (see Section Thirteen), works well to produce naturalistic effects in proscenium situations; it's almost impossible to use in the round. Dance lighting, low and from the side, works well only on proscenium or, in special circumstances, traverse stages.

Representational and Presentational Spaces

Beyond audience-stage relationships there are two perspectives from which to approach the question of space in the theatre. The first is representational and the second presentational.

Representational space is itself of two types. The first is *diegetic*—the space that we see on stage that represents places within the fictional world of the show: the kitchen, the Forest of Arden, the heath, the ship's cabin, and so on. Often representational space is clearly defined by a built set that resembles more or less realistically the space in which the fictional action takes place. But sets often only gesture in a stylized way to the places they represent, and sometimes the presence of walls, doors, furnishings, or forests are established purely by conventions that need to be made clear to actors and audiences and adhered to throughout the process unless there is a very specific reason for not doing so. Once an audience accepts that there is a wall between two stage spaces, it can be disconcerting to see an actor walk through it.

A second type of representational space is off stage (*extra-diegetic*). Extra-diegetic spaces are ones to which actors refer indexically, toward which they gesture, from which they enter, and into which they exit. These, again, must be clearly established and adhered to in all but the most absurdist productions. Once it has been established that the stage left exit leads to the garden, stage right to the village, and upstage centre to the bedroom, it is very confusing when someone exits up centre with a shovel (unless unusual sexual proclivities are being indexed).

If representational space is fixed and confined to the fictional world of the play, *presentational space* is a wild card, and can be extremely useful for a director. Presentational space is fluid and unfixed and tends to be associated with the present tense of performance rather than the past of the represented action. Although it's possible, and sometimes very useful, to associate some presentational areas of the stage with a particular character, emotion, or action—a place, for example, from which a central character or narrator delivers monologues, or a choric figure sets the scene—non-representational space can show up anywhere at any time. It can be evoked every time an actor turns out to the audience, winks, or delivers an aside, and it can be used deliberately to shatter the illusion, to comment on the action, or to engage the audience at a different, more self-conscious level. It is the natural home of irony.

More important, perhaps, than the distinction between representational and presentational space is the way in which you work with both relationally, using them together to shift the audience's focus, heighten or release tension, and construct a potentially complex and compelling relationship with a more, or less knowing audience. But the shifts between the two must be made with precision or audiences can become confused and lose focus.

Blocking

Thinking about blocking begins in meetings with your set designer and particularly in discussions about the floor plan, which can dictate in advance the show's patterns of movement (figure 7a).

Once the floor plan has been agreed upon, some directors work with the maquette (set model built to scale) to do a rough early blocking, determining entrances, exits, and general patterns of movement, before starting rehearsals. Others give the actors their heads and allow blocking to evolve throughout rehearsals. The advantage of the former method, particularly with a large cast, is to free the actors from having to think about where they're going and allow them to focus on more important things; the advantage of the latter is that it allows all movement to emerge naturally from motivations and relationships as they evolve in rehearsal.

If you do decide to "pre-block," it's best to let the cast know that this blocking is just provisional and that they're allowed, even encouraged, to follow their impulses and (provisionally) change the blocking as the show develops.

When blocking in a rehearsal hall in which the configurations and particularly vertical levels of the eventual set are not replicated, it's important to work with a maquette at hand in order to see, in three dimensions, the impact of what you're doing.

Blocking transitions between scenes should also be considered early on, at least in a preliminary way. Director Robert Lepage is reputed to have said that ninety percent of the

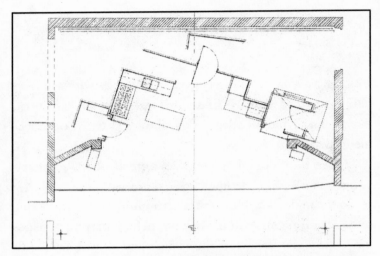

Figure 7a: A typical floor plan for a proscenium stage, showing entrances, exits, set pieces, and furnishings that shape movement patterns, in this case privileging a free flow to and from downstage left of centre, while creating a "trap" upstage right.

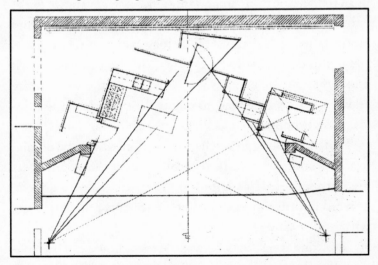

Figure 7b: The same floor plan showing sightlines, revealing what audience members on the extreme edges of the auditorium can see.

effectiveness of theatre relies on transitions, and though this is a bit of an overstatement, it's not without merit.

Scene-to-scene transitions can be handled in a variety of ways, most of which now involve some combination of movement, music or sound, and light, all of which have a huge impact on the rhythm and mood of a show, and all of which need to be rehearsed as much as the rest of the show and performed with as much precision. Many shows are destroyed by lengthy brownouts in which crew or stage management clumsily moves props, furnishings, and set pieces while the show's energy dissipates, the mood dissolves, and the audience chats among themselves.

In the contemporary theatre where the use of curtains is rare, it's often best to choreograph or block scene changes carefully and have them performed by the actors, who are sensitive to the moods and rhythms of the moment. The best transitions are entertaining in themselves and often can be part of the magic of a show.

Stage Picture

One function of blocking is the creation of stage picture: what the audience sees. Blocking for the stage picture involves arrangements, movements, tableaux, and so on that are pleasant, provocative, or meaningful for audiences in something like the ways that visual art is, or film, and it requires an eye for composition and a capacity for the achievement of focus (making sure that the audience is looking at what you want them to).

Initial considerations have to do with sightlines, taking constant care to make sure that everyone in the house has a good and unobstructed view of the stage (figure 7b). This means watching the developing show from all points in the house as you rehearse (or having an assistant director do so), and it can often mean actors' "cheating out"—adjusting their natural positioning to be sure that they can be seen properly and are not blocking the audience's view of other actors. In non-proscenium arrangements, the entries to vomitoria or audience aisles can often be strategically used to avoid blocking sightlines, as can levels and steps.

Focus means finding ways to ensure that the audience is paying attention to that part of the stage where meaningful action is happening. This can sometimes be achieved through lighting, but most of it is accomplished through the effective movements and positionings of the actors. Each type of

Figure 8: Blocking for focus on a proscenium stage.

stage has its own weaker or stronger positions (vertical and horizontal) to which the eye is more or less naturally drawn.

On a proscenium, especially on a raked stage, centre stage or upstage centre is the position of pre-eminent strength, followed by upstage right, and movements from up right to down left, at least in cultures in which the eye moves from left to right while reading, tend to convey strength and determination. Downstage left, close to the audience, otherwise a weak position, is an excellent spot for choric asides and commentaries.

On a thrust stage, centre (or better, balcony front-and-centre) functions as the hot spot.

In both proscenium and thrust configurations, downstage centre is an excellent position if the actor is alone on a stage, where she might otherwise be "upstaged" by someone behind her (the origin of the term) whose presence will immediately draw the eye.

Figure 9: Blocking for focus on a thrust stage.

Effective positioning in traverse and in-the-round arrangements tends more frequently to be determined by levels and by the strategic arrangement of actors and furnishings. In these as well as in thrust configurations a director has to make sure that whenever possible all audience members are able to see at least one actor's face at all times.

Knowledge of the stage's strongest positionings is an invaluable tool, but it's important not to rely on these too heavily because doing so will soon become boring: save them for key moments.

Otherwise focus can be achieved in a variety of ways. One is through the positioning of actors in groups that work to direct audiences' attention. A huddle of actors upstage right on a proscenium looking intently at (or even pointing toward) a solo actor down centre will ensure that if the audience's gaze wanders it will be redirected appropriately (figure 8). A similar effect can be achieved on a thrust stage with actors distributed around the edge of the thrust, looking toward the stage centre action (figure 9).

Another key tool for the achievement of focus is the strategic use of stillness, or of movement that draws the eye. This can range from large, cross-stage sweeps that function like a camera's pan to refocus audience attention by drawing the eye from one side of the stage to the other, to the use of frenetic downstage movement that is set in contrast to the stillness of a solo figure upstage. Depending on the context, either movement or stillness can draw the eye: stillness is powerful on an otherwise busy stage; movement is compelling when all else is still.

It's even possible to make use of something as small as a tiny gesture on an otherwise still stage, which can make the audience focus on a single detail with the same effectiveness as a camera's close-up. Indeed, the flicker of an eyelash will be the centre of focus on an otherwise still body on an otherwise still stage. A smile from the same actor will broaden the focus to her head, a gesture with her arm will broaden it further to her upper body, a subsequent movement of her foot to her entire body, and so on. As other actors begin gradually to move, the eye, like a camera, will zoom out for a wide-angle view of the whole stage.

Stage composition is the art of making each moment on the stage look good (or look bad in strategic ways) and perhaps more importantly of communicating meaning and emotion visually. Initial rules of thumb involve avoiding static images, which usually involve arranging actors in straight lines that are parallel or perpendicular to the front or sides of the stage (in the case of proscenium, thrust, or traverse configurations). They also involve avoiding compositions that are meaninglessly or distractingly imbalanced while keeping things dynamic (not letting them becoming boringly or predictably balanced).

Often productive tensions can be initiated and resolved by playing *against* a stage's positions of strength or by strategic imbalances among the company that may or may not move toward resolution, in much the same way as a cadence in a piece of music functions by resolving discord into harmony or leaving an element of dissonant suspense.

Creating meaningful stage pictures always means paying attention to, reinforcing, qualifying or even playing deliberately against the mood of a scene through the use of line, weight, and movement. You also need to pay attention to the ways in which the colour, cut, and style of costumes work in relation to one another and to the set and lighting in any given scene or grouping of actors. A yellow dress will pull focus in the most blandly organized group of brown-hued chorus members.

Blocking can also say a great deal about the relationships among the characters, which characters naturally gravitate toward one another, which tend to be isolated, which tend to be in oppositional relationships to one another (as can be indicated by sharp angles), and which circle one another (playfully, for example, or as hunter to prey). And blocking can be indicative of a character's or characters' relationship to the (scenic, stage) environment, their level of comfort or unease, both in general (is this place one they feel at home in?) and in relation to specific areas of the environment (is the character drawn to the bar or the basement, the fish tank or the futon, the kitchen or the catamaran)?

Blocking and Proxemics

Proxemics refers to spatial factors in human relationships. In the theatre it means proximity or distance between the actors, between the actors and the environment, and between the actors and the audience.

Much of your time with the actors in rehearsal will involve privately keeping the stage picture in mind while working with the cast on the physicality of their onstage relationships and on how spatialization feeds the actors' imaginations, emotions, and energies. These include predominantly such things as personal space, comfort zones, sexually charged space, and status relationships.

To work effectively with proxemics means paying close attention to the dynamics between actors and characters as felt relationships that charge a scene and give it much of its affective emotional clout. You need to be sensitive in rehearsal to the ways in which such tensions between bodies ebb and flow as actors' proximity increases and decreases, as they face one-another or turn away, and as they come into contact.

A scene can often be highly charged at those moments when two actors come near to touching, and tension can be dissipated when they actually make contact. An actor can seem to exert a magnetic, almost gravitational pull by strategically turning or moving away from another actor, creating a particularly intense moment, or can create an aura of intimidation through stillness or through the invasion of another's personal space.

Attention to such matters can be used effectively to raise the stakes in a scene. Think, for example, of interrogation scenes in which a standing actor circles upstage behind a seated figure, invading her personal space without becoming physically visible to her. Or think of moments in which an intimate gesture across an impossible distance creates poignant intimations of yearning or loss.

Physical relationships between actors who are standing and sitting, near and far, public and private, can involve complex dynamics of shifting status or shifting degrees of intimacy or distance, as can varying combinations of movement and stillness, and subtle gestural vocabularies can reveal a great deal. As a director in rehearsal you have to learn to be as

sensitive to such spatial and gestural relationships as to vocal inflection, and bodily rhythms can communicate at least
as much as verbal ones.

10. STYLIZED MOVEMENT

Choreography is the provenance of dance and musical theatre, which is beyond the scope of this short book, but there
has been an increasing and healthy trend in all but the most
naturalistic contemporary theatre toward the use of what I
call a movement designer—someone whose work is situated
somewhere between blocking and choreography and who
works closely with the actors and director of a show to develop, implement, and refine the show's movement vocabulary.
Everything I have said about communication with designers
in Section Four applies to communicating with movement
designers: you need to develop an imagistic and metaphorical vocabulary for communicating your sense of the feel of
the show without dictating specific ideas about particular
movements. And you need to be collaborative in practice,
providing specific feedback on what the designer comes up
with without dictating its terms.

There are several approaches to movement design, but if
a movement designer's work is to be fully integrated into the
process, s/he should work alongside the show's composer and/
or sound designer and be fully familiar with the tones and
rhythms of the show as it develops, particularly if it's using a
full soundscape or score (see Section Thirteen).

Similarly, the movement designer should be involved along with you as director, together with the sound and lighting designers, to work on the show's scene-by-scene transitions. As I've indicated elsewhere, transitions are hugely important in shaping a work and creating its rhythms, and stylized movement can work together with sound, music, and light to create effective and meaningful transitions that are part of, rather than pauses in, a show. Rhythm is crucial in all aspects of directing, and individual movements and gestures, or entire transitions, can be timed much in the way that a called cue has a count and can happen in a snap, a fade, a melt, or a morphing depending on the effect one wants to achieve.

Some approaches to movement design simply involve finding or developing exercises to help individual actors find their characters' bodies. Examples of these include:

1. Having actors identify, in one word, one or more central aspects of the characters they are playing, and then snap into a shape that embodies that word, after which the body can be mobilized—working out how it stands, sits, walks, runs, and so on, emerging from and retreating to a basic shape. This exercise can be used in naturalistic productions to help actors embody characters or in productions in which actors play roles from anywhere in or outside of nature, and it can be executed with whatever degree of subtlety or exaggeration is appropriate to the style of the show.

2. Once fundamental character work has been done, asking the actors individually (and in isolation from one another) to walk in a circle, putting them through calming exercises that help them to relax into their own naturalized ways of carrying themselves.

Once this is done, as the actors continue to walk, either you or the movement designer asks them silently to notice what parts of their bodies they're leading with, where their centres of gravity are, what their natural rhythms are, and where they hold their tension.

The actors are talked into character as they continue to walk, talking them through any backstory that has been developed, and into the situation that they are in and the feelings and desires that they have at that moment of the play. As this happens and the characters begin to be realized, the actors' bodies will begin to change subtly and slowly into those of their characters.

Once this is achieved, the actors (still walking) are asked to notice, once again, what parts of their bodies they are now leading with, where their centres of gravity are, what their natural rhythms are, and where they hold their tension.

Having silently taken note of these, the actors are then asked, still walking, gradually to exaggerate these qualities, pushing eventually to the point of caricature: if they lead with their foreheads, they need to extend their foreheads to an extreme degree;

if they are centred in their hips, they need exaggerat-edly to settle their weight there; if their rhythms are quick and slightly askew to their right side, they need to speed up still more and exaggerate their irregulari-ties; if they hold their tension between their shoulder blades, they need to become extremely taut there. After walking in these caricatures for a time, they are asked to relax back in to the more comfortable bodies of their characters, and finally, still walking, to relax back in to their own bodies.

All of this should be followed by a discussion of the exercise, making sure that the actors are made fully conscious of choices that they may have made unconsciously and drawing attention to significant discoveries.

The result is that the actors not only develop their characters' bodies, but also develop a short-hand method of getting into those bodies (proceeding quickly to the caricature and then relaxing back in to the body). The exercise seems at first to be profoundly naturalistic, but it can be used for almost any kind or degree of stylization as well, depending on how far (if at all) the relaxation back from caricature is taken.

These are simply two examples of many such exercises, and you'll no doubt develop your own, with or without a move-ment designer, depending on your needs, the project, and the actors you're working with.

Another method, most suitable for ensemble shows be-cause there is less focus on individual actors and the characters they embody, involves developing a *gestural vocabulary* for the entire company early in the process, a vocabulary that becomes available throughout.

In this approach the movement designer works with the actors and you as director to identify ideas, words, and themes that are central to the show, after which they work as a group, each actor developing a precise gesture involving the entire body that is associated with each word, idea, or theme. The actor who develops each gesture then breaks it down into constituent and numbered movements used to achieve that gesture and teaches it, by numbered parts, to the group as a whole.

Once a "bank" of gestural vocabulary has been built up to cover as broad a range of words, ideas, and themes as seems necessary, these movements are available to be used full out (if the scene or moment is highly stylized), or at some percentage thereof if the desired effect is more subtle. The developed gestures are useful at any point when you want certain words or concepts to "pop" in a scene, but they're also useful in creating specificity, clarity, and precision, avoiding gestural clutter or generalization, while at the same time uniting the company in a shared movement vocabulary.

These are only a few examples of how a movement designer might usefully be employed on a production. The variations are endless, and the particular approach will depend on the demands of the show and on the movement designer's own expertise and proclivities.

Whatever the approach, when a particular sequence involving stylized movement is being worked on, it's usually best to allow the movement designer to work with the actors, observing what they are doing closely and being available for consultation, but allowing the designer to do her or his work. Once a first version of a sequence is complete, you can then consult with the designer, tweaking it and shaping the work, taking some things further and pulling back on others, until it fits with the flow of the rest of the show and, of course, with the dialogue.

11. SCENE WORK AND PROBLEM-SOLVING

Scene Work

An ideal rehearsal process, rarely achieved, would mean doing scene work exclusively from just after first meeting to tech week, building in whatever order or organization (see Section Three) from work on small units to whole scenes to whole acts and finally to runs, tech rehearsals, dress rehearsals, and previews. The first couple of work-throughs of all of the scenes in a full-length show may take (say) a week each, while the second may take a couple of days, the third, a day, and then you're into working on one act at a time, and so on.

When doing scene work, it's usually best to let a moment play itself out the first time through before interrupting; after that, it's best to let actors know in advance that you *will* be interrupting. But you need to build on what they're doing, not what you imagine or have decided in advance that they should be doing. This means extremely close observation and listening, which are a director's most important skills.

Try to see actors' impulses, including (especially) the ones they don't act on, and create a space that allows them to follow those impulses. Actors, particularly in the early stages, censor themselves, when their instinctive responses are often the most powerful. Allow the actors their own individual processes and learn how to work with and talk to each one individually.

Once you see what the actors give you, you can then enhance certain aspects of their work through adjustments to movement, positioning, and so on. Often it's useful to raise the stakes in a scene by shifting the situation or given circumstances in such a way as to make their choices more urgent. This can involve suggesting to actors that their motivations should have to do less with what they happen to want and more with what they feel they *need*. Sometimes it's helpful to provide the actors with "biz," something to do that takes the pressure off of too intense a concentration on their text, but this shouldn't be overdone to the degree that the show becomes overly "bizzy."

Much of your work, though, will be on helping the actors make what they do more specific, more precise, more simple, and more clear. This often means encouraging them to work in smaller units in the first instance, finding more detailed motivations, and especially more specific—and often more frequent—*thought changes*.

Although many actors will have learned to divide scenes into "beats"—coherent units of action (see Section One)—for me the thought change is the most basic unit of acting. It's the moment at which a character has a new motive, a new idea about *how* to get what s/he wants, a change of mind, or a new impulse. Thought changes don't necessarily coincide with beats as units of action, or with grammar or punctuation (and empty pauses at the end of a phrase or a sentence while an actor finds new motivation are anathema). Often the most interesting things happen when a thought change occurs in mid-thought (or mid-sentence)—though this should not become self-indulgent or mannered.

Lines aren't the only things that have to be motivated. Scene work always coincides with the implementation, development, and coordination of blocking, and thought changes motivate and subtend movement and gesture on or between lines as well as the lines themselves. Much of scene work involves helping the actors to find or motivate their blocking, to coordinate their movements and gestures so that they're providing motivation to one another. One actor's turning away or tuning out, for example, can make another actor work harder to achieve her objective, increasing her motivation and raising the stakes.

Inevitably some beats, units, or scenes need more work than others, either because they're inherently difficult, or crucial to the play, or because you have run into unexpected problems (see below), so it's important to dedicate some time in the rehearsal schedule for scene work "to be announced" (TBA).

The early stages of scene work are concerned with working in small units, exploring possibilities, and finding options. They often involve either asking actors to try various things out or following suggestions that they or others make in order to see what works best. At this stage the pace tends to be slow, actors take time to find their motivations, and rehearsals can consist in time-consuming negotiations across different embodied understandings of what's going on. This stage can also often be one of making exciting and unanticipated discoveries; for a director this can be the most rewarding part of the process.

As decisions about motivation and movement become increasingly fixed and you begin to work in larger units, the pace should pick up and all but the most significant *full* pauses (pauses in which something *happens*) should gradually be eliminated. This doesn't, however, mean asking actors to deliver their lines more quickly; it usually *does* involve asking them to *think* faster—to think *on* a line or movement rather than before it.

By the time you're doing uninterrupted run-throughs, you're doing so in order, first, to get a larger sense of the show's shape, rhythm, and stage picture so that you can adjust them. This means paying attention to whether the show's turning points are sufficiently pointed, its patterns sufficiently clear, its pace sufficiently and appropriately varied, and its blocking and look sufficiently varied and compelling.

A second reason for doing run-throughs is to identify scenes or moments that need more close scene work and problem-solving during rehearsals.

A third reason is to allow the actors to become comfortable and familiar with the sequencing of the scenes, and the final reason is to allow you to give notes. Notes should be used sparingly if at all until the point where you are doing complete runs. Until then it's usually better to work on the moment *in* the moment.

Notes should be given in person whenever possible, usually to the entire cast. On rare occasions when a note needs to be given in private to an individual actor, particularly if it is a lengthy one, it shouldn't be given while the whole company is sitting around watching or wasting its time and resenting it; in this case it should be saved for scheduled TBA slots.

Take a break after a run before starting a note session and start with general notes that apply to everyone (on things like pacing, size, projection, energy, ensemble, and so on). Then work through the show giving notes scene by scene. Make sure everyone has the script and a pencil.

Try where possible to give positive rather than negative notes; that is, preface a note with "try doing . . . " rather than "don't do . . . " And try in note sessions to give more or less equal weight to everyone, so that they all feel they are getting feedback and no one feels picked on, singled out, or left out.

Problem-Solving

There are a wide variety of problems that inevitably emerge in scene work in any rehearsal process. The actors in a scene may make choices that are incompatible with one another. Any actor may not be managing to make a choice that works, or isn't understanding something, or is overcomplicating, overcompensating, or blocked. One or more scenes may be unconvincing, awkward, boring.

There are various ways in which such problems and others can be addressed, but they *should* be addressed *with* the actors in the first instance, and usually by going back to basics.

Bad directors, or directors working with too little time, will often resort to covering up problems, hiding the fact that an actor doesn't know what s/he's saying by adding some business, throwing in a dazzling effect, upstaging an awkward moment with something more interesting, or otherwise distracting the audience's attention. You need to avoid this.

Going back to basics can often mean simply sitting down with the actors and making sure that everyone has done the same script work—that everyone recognizes the same beats and units, knows why they are saying and doing what they're saying and doing, and knows where their thought changes are.

This might mean something as basic as dividing each speech into thought units and insisting that the actors say their subtext before they say their line or before they move. This might mean saying out loud sequences such as these, with text preceded by spoken subtext:

"(*I want to attack*) 'Hi, how lovely to see you.' "

"(*I want to apologize*) 'Please . . . ' (*I want to desta-bilize*) 'sit . . . ' (*I want to surprise!*) 'here!' (*I want to insult*) 'That chair is far too narrow for someone of your . . . ' (*I want to humiliate*) 'stature.' "

Again, note that thought changes can happen in mid-sentence. They can happen without anything being said, but will manifest in movement, gesture, or expression.

Note too that problems can sometimes be solved by merely increasing the stakes in the motivation. If an actor is using "I want to relax," for example, upping the ante by shifting to "I want to escape" might just solve the problem of a boring scene.

Other techniques for problem-solving can involve various kinds of games, improvisations, or other techniques.

Games shouldn't be used without a specific and clear purpose. Games can be whatever you make up, but they are usually most useful at the outset of a rehearsal process and are used around doing introductions or creating an ensemble.

Introductory games might involve such things as name games (pointing to and naming people across a circle by turns, and in rapid succession, for example), bio games (two-minute meetings with the person in the cast you least know, followed by introductions of one another to the group).

Ensemble-building games might include things like trust exercises, listening games, or mirror games.

Use your imagination, but there are a wide variety of books with theatre games, including notably Viola Spolin's *Theater Games for Rehearsal: A Director's Handbook* and Augusto Boal's *Games for Actors and Non-Actors*. Some of these specific games are useful during scene work, usually when they involve unlocking blocked actors or shifting atmospheres that aren't working, but it's rare that a more generalized or expansive game is useful once scene work is underway.

Improvisation can be a very useful problem-solving tool, but again, it shouldn't be used without a clear and specific purpose. Purposes can include such things as:

Helping to develop and negotiate backstory when it's either not clear or in conflict with those of other characters. This can involve such things as asking actors to improvise, in character, the first time they met, or any key, crucial, or crisis point in their background that they have to come to an agreement on.

Exploring the characters' worlds outside of the on-stage action when they bear on the scenes you're working on. This can involve improvising scenes from the characters' offstage life at home, at work, or in society more generally.

Negotiating and clarifying relationships (including status relationships, social relationships, and physical relationships) among a group. This can involve asking the company to attend a party or social event or meeting together and seeing what relationships develop, what groups form, who becomes isolated, and who assumes the spotlight or takes control.

Exploring a character's inner life. This can involve using "hot-seat" exercises to discover more about a character's intellectual, psychological, emotional, spiritual lives, together with their affiliations, alliances, tastes, preferences, and so on. Hot-seat exercises involve an actor, in character, responding spontaneously in the first person to questions about themselves posed by the rest of the company.

Grounding a scene in a "real-world" context. This might mean rehearsing a barroom scene in a real barroom, a bus scene on a real bus. This is particularly useful if one or more of the actors is unfamiliar with the context in which the action takes place.

Negotiating a story arc. This might, for example, involve using tableaux of "where we are now" and "where we end up," and then improvising how they got there.

Other techniques can also be used to break logjams in your own or the actors' thinking and vision by, for example:

Changing the given circumstances, the time of day, the location, or other context of a scene that's not working.

Temporarily reassigning roles so that actors can see others in their parts—though it is important to be careful not to let this turn into actors giving one another notes, and not to let it become competitive.

Assigning physical tasks that take the pressure off the text ("speak your monologue while washing the dishes").

Asking actors to perform the scene

a) Without words, in order to focus on expressive physicality.

b) Without movement, in order to focus on voice.

c) In gobbledegook, which can often valuably reveal intention and motivation as the actors struggle to communicate what they want.

d) In their own words.

Asking the actors to perform the scene in a more intimate context, or in a loud and crowded room, or in fear of being overheard, or across a vast distance, or over a phone, or in whispers. This last is a good physical exercise anyway, which can often reveal unexpected emotion by putting pressure on the diaphragm.

In almost every case it's essential, after an improvisation or exercise is complete, to talk through *briefly* with the company what may have been gained and what discoveries were made, drawing attention to what was useful and what was not, before *immediately* returning to work on the scene or moment, applying the discoveries made and moving on.

12. MAKING DECISIONS, NARROWING CHOICES, REFINING SCOPE

I think of a rehearsal process as a kind of reverse or inverted hourglass, where the first half, more or less, is about opening up, gathering as much information and as many options and possibilities as you can, expanding the horizons and discovering things that you hadn't known were available, and the second half is about making choices.

This first half is all exploratory and exciting, involving research, improvisation, and open-ended scene work. This is also the most collaborative period, when input from everyone is important and welcome, and when it's always worth trying out an idea, suggestion, or impulse. And many totally unexpected things can happen during this period that fully inform the production.

The second half of the process is different and involves making an accumulation of decisions that sequentially limit future options, narrow the field, and increasingly refine the scope of the show. It's important to learn to recognize when it's time to start making such decisions and to know the ways in which decisions once made delimit future choices. Made too early such decisions can unnecessarily limit the show's potential and richness; made too late and actors and designers can become overly invested in things that need to be left behind, and indeed actors can sometimes have trouble shedding them.

It's also important to recognize and accept directorial responsibility at this stage: this is where the limits of collaboration can become apparent and responsibility becomes more centralized.

Clearly, of course, decisions *are* made from the outset of the process that almost immediately delimit future choices: the choice of project or script, design decisions, casting, and so on, but once these have provided a context, explorations can begin again. Equally clearly, there are decisions that must be made in order for the show to go into tech week: if the lighting designer isn't able to see a show in which blocking is more or less finalized, she's unlikely to be able to provide a very precise lighting plot. If the pacing of the show isn't relatively fixed, a composer or sound designer is unlikely to be able to provide appropriate cues, and timings will only be approximate.

At some point actors, too, have to make more or less fixed choices about characters, motivations, units of action and thought. It's only rarely that actors can surprise one another productively in performance or even in the late stages of a rehearsal process—though this can happen and can keep things fresh. It's important to know when it can or cannot be encouraged.

As director you have to know three things:

1. When a final decision needs to be made and when it can productively be delayed. Don't feel pressure to make a decision if you aren't ready to. If you are

hesitant there's probably a reason, and you won't lose face by saying "I don't know yet."

2. What the right decision is. If you've done your homework this will usually be crystal clear and you should instinctively know the right choice. Try to follow your instincts at this stage rather than over-analyzing or trying to do something clever.

3. What the implications of any given decision are for all subsequent choices. If you make a certain decision about a prop, for example, this will determine what can be done with that prop, depending on how heavy it is, how flexible or fragile it is, how ungainly it is, and so on. The same is true of a costume choice, or of a movement.

But the need to know the implications of a decision also applies to less obvious and less physical choices. If you've found particular turning points in the action, particular key motivations, particular rhythms, these will all predetermine to a greater or lesser extent what you can subsequently do, and this needs to be understood and anticipated or you can end up choosing yourself into a directorial corner.

As you move into the final stages of rehearsal as director you have to begin to function more and more as a surrogate audience in the rehearsal process, standing back, as it were, and seeing through the future audiences' eyes to work out what's clear and what isn't, what "works" and what doesn't, what's exciting and what's boring, and whether the show is communicating what you want it to. This means cultivating the capacity to be genuinely surprised and moved by things that you already know or have seen many times. It means cultivating the capacity to "read" the performance (as opposed to the script) with genuinely fresh eyes.

This is also a period when as director you will begin to eliminate flab and pare things down to essentials. Decisions made during this period should generally be strong and bold, often surprising, often theatrical. They'll often involve increasing the stakes while also increasing the detail and specificity of every element, from the placement of a chair, to a costume detail, to the tiniest gesture. They also often involve having the courage to cut or begin again with sequences that aren't working, are unclear, or are cumbersome. However good an idea may have been in the beginning, if it isn't doing what it was meant to do it needs to be rethought or let go.

The good side of all of this is that if you're making informed and strong decisions everyone involved will be able to see and experience a show that's moving toward clarity and precision and is getting increasingly powerful. Everyone will become more confident and will themselves begin to make clearer and stronger choices as everything is ratcheted up a notch.

13. WORKING WITH SOUND, LIGHT, AND PROJECTIONS (AND SMELL, TOUCH, AND TASTE)

It's important to remember that light, sound, and projections don't operate in isolation from one another, or from anything else in a show. Cues for sound, light, and projection, however, very often come together or in close proximity to one another, and they can be used to enhance one another's effects. And of course projections depend upon light levels and angles to be visible.

Sound

It's crucial that you start thinking about and planning for sound early. In fact, it's ideal where possible to have a sound designer with a laptop in rehearsals throughout, with sound functioning in the room virtually as another actor in the creation process. And of course a sound designer should be treated like any other designer (see Section Four), not simply as a technician who provides sound effects that you want.

There are two basic, sometimes overlapping ways to think about and use sound (and music):

1. *Sound effects*: This means collecting sound from databases, sound effects CDs, or creating or recording

the sounds that are called for in the piece (car doors closing, gunshots, phones ringing, the bark of a dog, a radio playing off stage), and calling them as cues during the show.

Sound effects can be naturalistic (a real car door closing), atmospheric (the sound of frogs and cicadas), symbolic (a door slams and reverberates as the sign of all options ending), or any combination of these.

These types of sound have an impact on actors as well as audiences, so they shouldn't be introduced into rehearsals too late: give actors a chance to use them and to get used to them, and if at all possible build sound cues into the stage manager's prompt book as you proceed through the rehearsal process.

2. *Soundscape*: Think film. A soundscape is a more or less continuous sonic and/or musical underscoring throughout the play, though it's usually combined with called sound effects.

The soundscape itself may be timed rather than called, or may be called in sequences that coincide with scenes or other units. It can consist of sounds or music or both, and like sound effects can be naturalistic, atmospheric, symbolic, or some combination of these.

One of the opportunities a soundscape provides is periods of silence that can be very effective at creating tension, or stillness, or a sense of emptiness. Precisely because the audience has become accustomed to continuous sound, silence can be experienced as a sound cue.

Sound and music can be live or recorded. If live, they can be created by the cast, by live onstage musicians, by a musician performing off stage, or by a sound designer/operator working live from the booth on a computer. Each of these has its advantages and disadvantages. As a general rule, however, pre-recorded sound dictates the timing for everything else; performed live it becomes part of a more spontaneous onstage interaction.

It's important to consider the style of other elements of a show in considering whether you want to use naturalistic or somehow stylized sound, whether you want to use music (with or without a source that's explainable in naturalistic terms), and so on. The style of a soundscape, or of musical underscoring, can complement or deliberately work against the show's acting style or those of its set, costume, or lighting design, and decisions about this need to be made early on in the process.

Sound and music have a number of uses, including:

1. *Defining place and space*: This can involve naturalistic sounds—traffic and street noises indicate that the action takes place in a city, frogs and cicadas indicate a rural area, surf sounds a seaside, and so on. Bird sounds can even be used to indicate geographical areas where specific birds are found, and you have to be careful with this in a naturalistic production

because there are bound to be birders in the audience who will let you know if you get it wrong.

The volume of space can also usefully be defined through things like reverb and echo, which differentiate usefully between enclosed spaces, large rooms, and outdoors. Even the regularity or absorbency of imagined surfaces and walls can be suggested by using reverb units: the reverberations are very different in a rock-walled cave, for example, than in a padded cell or a room of the same size with concrete walls.

Finally, weather and atmospheric conditions can be communicated in part through sound. On a bright, clear day sound travels crisply over considerable distances and reverberates; fog, or especially snow, have a muffling effect.

2. *Communicating information to audiences*: A phone's ringing, a train's going by, it's raining outside, a car's arriving. Sound can also be used to help tell the story: one of the most famous moments in western theatre history, the door slamming at the end of Ibsen's *A Doll's House*, is a sound cue.

3. *Creating atmosphere and mood*: Both sound and music can do a great deal to set the mood of a scene or the atmosphere of a place much in the way that it does in film and television, and it can do so in ways that are overt (as when swelling music creates suspense or indicates impending disaster, or when "light" music gives the audience permission to laugh).

But sound can also work subtly, or even subliminally, as when sound at a low level effectively sets a tone without the audience being consciously aware that they're hearing anything.

4. *Supporting actors*: Often a scene can be enhanced through the use of sound to help actors out by reinforcing the mood that they want to create, by creating empathy, by establishing a particular rhythm, or even by creating a productive obstacle for an actor to struggle against. Think of how the noise of a crowded public area can reinforce an urgent need to communicate, particularly in intimate scenes.

5. *Shaping structure and rhythm, and marking transitions*: Sound, or more specifically music, together with lighting, is often used to mark transitions between acts, scenes, or structural divisions, to indicate passage of time, changes of place, and perhaps more importantly changes of mood.

It's helpful to develop a sound vocabulary for communicating with sound designers and composers. Some of the most useful terms include:

1. *Volume*: This works in many ways that are obvious, but some of its less obvious functions have to do with the audience's relationship to the performance. High levels, for example, can push an audience back in their seats, encouraging detachment or a kind of

consumerism, while low levels can sometimes work productively to invite the audience in. At extremes, however, both can also be annoying, particularly if they aren't well coordinated with the actors' voices.

You may also want to use the language, borrowed from music, of crescendos (sound levels increasing) and diminuendos (decreasing) in communicating what you want.

2. *Direction*: Decisions about what direction the sound should come from will affect the physical placement of speakers (front of house? upstage? wings? overhead? beneath the risers?). Directional sound can provide information about where a visiting car is arriving from, where the nearby highway is, what's going on upstairs, or any number of things. It can also provide special effects, as when a helicopter takes off, circles the space, and departs to the east.

Direction can also have an emotional impact. Sound emanating from upstage alone tends to be associated only with the fictional world, and is often less powerful or empathic than surround sound or sound that comes from behind and/or beneath the audience, where the vibrations of bass notes, in particular, can have a visceral effect.

3. *Pitch*: A high-pitched sound clearly has a very different resonance than a deep bass, and as this suggests, terms borrowed from music's bass and treble

can again be useful in discussing it. The feel of a taut, high-pitched violin string can create a very different kind of tension than a low-pitched organ drone.

4. *Rhythm* and *tempo*: Rhythm and tempo can be major components of setting the pace and shape of a show. It would be useful for you to develop a way of talking about regularities and irregularities in a show's rhythm. Again, borrowing from music can help—using the language of 3/4, 4/4, or 6/8 time, talking about syncopation (where the emphasis falls off of the regular beat), or talking about the feel of various dance rhythms, from waltz, through tango to reggae, disco, or hip hop.

Rhythm, of course, generally works with tempo. A similar rhythm has a very different feel when taken at a different speed, as when reggae accelerated turns quickly into dance music.

5. *Timbre*: This has to do with attack and decay and is key to what a sound actually sounds like—to why a clarinet sounds different from a trumpet, for example. Reference to musical instruments can be useful in communicating about timbre: the growl of a tenor saxophone has a very different timbre than the whistle of a piccolo.

6. *Texture*: This is related to timbre but can have a more direct kinesthetic impact. Texture has to do with whether the sound is throaty, pure, rough, or

nasal. Texture is what differentiates fingernails on a blackboard from the sound of running water, and as in these examples can produce quite visceral effects. (Try to avoid using running water, for example, unless intermission looms.)

Texture has to do not only with the source of sounds but also with the context in which they're received, since the acoustic makeup of an auditorium can muffle sounds, brighten them, disperse them, or produce echoes. And of course large audiences can often muffle or dampen the brightest of soundscapes.

Pre-show music works to prepare the audience for the show in much the same way as programs and promotional materials do, but it's important not to anticipate or pre-empt the show. While setting the mood it's usually not wise to use music from the show itself, or even to use music that's too powerful in its impact. Sometimes it's best to use no music at all.

Intermission music bridges acts, and though it's often not consciously heard beneath the buzz of audiences, if used carefully it can subliminally shift the tone from one act to the next. Post-show music should pick up on the mood of the show's ending while supporting the curtain call. This means that a certain rhythm is very helpful—one that underscores applause but that nevertheless has to be quite different in tragedies than comedies.

Sound for musicals is usually more complicated than for non-musical theatre and can involve a complex plotting of microphones, microphone levels, monitors, and a sound board where mixing takes place. Detailed consideration of directing for musical theatre is beyond the scope of this book, but if you do take on a musical, make sure you have a sound operator with musical theatre experience, make sure you have the right equipment, and make sure you have enough tech time.

Light

Again, it's best to have lighting in mind from the outset of your discussions with set and costume designers (if they are different from the lighting designer). If you're thinking in scenographic ways (in which one scenographer designs sets and lights—and often costumes), light is a key piece and is the scenographer's responsibility.

In an ideal world a lighting designer playing with a portable board and rudimentary instrument hang throughout the rehearsal process would be best, though this is rarely ever possible. But it's crucial that a lighting designer be invited as early as possible to a run of the show (once blocking is more or less complete) in order to see what areas of the stage are being used and how. I've discussed how to talk with designers in Section Four, and those suggestions apply equally to lighting designers, including treating the designer as a full collaborator in the vision of the show.

There are different ways to think about lighting a show, but in almost every case the priority is making sure that the audience can see the actors' faces. Beyond that it's again a question of style. There are two basic lighting styles that most designs play variations on, plus an infinite variety of stylizations:

1. McCandless, or *three-point lighting* (figure 10), has become standard for naturalistic lighting on a proscenium stage. This involves two primary lights coming from opposite directions about 45° above and on either side of the actors, one with more intensity than the other and one cooler in colour than the other, plus usually a top or back light. Sometimes this is supplemented with some footlighting or other fill. Over the years, this system has evolved into five- and six-point lighting to increase fill and flexibility.

Colours in this method tend to favour amber and blue. Naturalistic lighting will often employ gobos (perforated steel plates) to break up the light or indicate window or other patterns.

2. *Dance lighting* (figure 11), on the other hand, is increasingly used in the theatre to feature sculpted bodies in space. It relies heavily on low-angled side lighting ranging from shin- to head-height (or just above), and is more minimalist and less fussy than the McCandless technique (though it usually also includes some back, front, and top light as fill).

Dance lighting can involve a wide range of hues for dance and movement pieces in particular, but in theatre often relies heavily on fairly clean, white light.

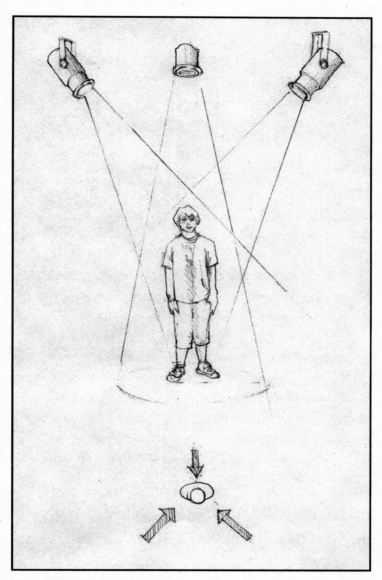

Figure 10: McCandless (three-point) lighting.

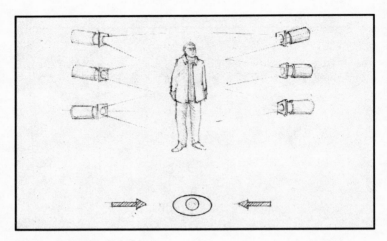

Figure 11: Dance lighting.

3. *Stylization* can take many forms, from surrealist through expressionist to minimalist (sometimes as minimal as a bare light bulb—as in much of Hillar Liitoja's work, or even the harshness of fluorescents—as in fu-GEN Theatre's highly successful production of Leon Aureus's *Banana Boys*). It can often involve a much wider range of colours, angles, and intensities than naturalistic lighting. If you plan to use any of the more exaggerated types of stylization, your lighting designer will be a crucial collaborator from the outset.

As with sound, it's helpful to develop a vocabulary for communicating with lighting designers. Some of the most useful terms include:

1. *Intensity* (or level): This is the brightness of the light. Bright lights tend to feel upbeat, and therefore tend to be used for comedy. Low levels can produce a brooding feel. Levels that are either too bright or too low can be irritating.

2. *Direction* and *angle*: These have to do with where the light is coming from in relation to what's being lit, ranging from backlight at waist level or above (which produces silhouettes) through various angles and heights to footlights (placed on the floor at the front of the stage), which on their own are dramatic but unflattering.

As indicated earlier, naturalistic lighting favours 45° angles above and to either side of actors, while dance lighting favours low-angled side light. Other unusual or startling effects can be achieved using bolder angles or backlights. Comedy tends to favour gentle angles (above 45°), tragedy sharper ones, which can produce long shadows while also emphasizing the threatening angularity of faces and other features.

3. *Colour*: Stage lighting achieves colour through the use of gels (tinted polycarbonate or polyester sheets). "Warm" (amber) light and "cool" (blue) light are the most frequently used colours because they imitate those of the natural world most closely.

The colour palette of a show can vary considerably, but comedies tend toward the warm, tragedies toward the cool; intimate scenes tend to be warm, more formal or conflicted scenes are cooler; indoor is usually warm, outdoor cooler except for early morning or late evening scenes when the sun is low on the horizon.

Other colours are used for special purposes, both naturalistic (candlelight, light reflected off of coloured surfaces, green light coming through a canopy of trees) and not (an expressionistic show might choose intensities of colours not generally found in nature).

4. *Texture*: This also has to do with saturation—the more colour saturation a gel has, the more texture the light takes on, especially at low levels. Think of Macbeth's line "light thickens" and you'll understand what texture means in relation to light.

Gobos are sometimes used to provide a different kind of texturing, creating a less regular beam of light in order to imitate light coming through trees, windows, or other filters. These "dappled" effects can quickly become clichéd, so use them sparingly. They are most effective on faces rather than floors. Gobos usually require a reasonably high level of intensity in order to be read.

5. *Focus and coverage*: There are many different kinds of lighting instruments, and they are usually distinguished from one another by their capacity to focus light where you want it. An unfocused light can be useful for broad washes but doesn't usually work

very well on its own for lighting faces or pulling the eyes of the audience to where you want them to look ("achieving focus").

Degrees of focus and coverage vary, and at times this has to do with hiding things—leaving some areas of the stage in darkness (without coverage). Again, comedy tends to favour broad coverage; tragedy can often be enhanced by dramatic pools or shafts of light.

6. *Count*: This refers to the length of time it takes from the moment a cue is called to the moment it reaches its final state, and it's a crucial tool. A very long count can accomplish a subtle mood change almost subconsciously, or a move from afternoon to evening to night, for example. A snap or a one-count can have enormous dramatic impact, and can also serve rhythmically to punctuate a show.

There are many different uses for lighting, some of them more obvious than others:

1. *Making things visible* (and invisible): Chiefly this is about lighting actors, but also sets and costumes.

It's sometimes tempting in tragedies or bleaker shows to underlight, but it's best to avoid this, at least for any length of time. Very low light levels give audiences headaches, and you eventually lose their attention if they can't see the actors' expressions clearly. Oddly, it's also much more difficult to hear an actor you can't see clearly. You can create the mood you're looking for through other means (shadows, angles, pools of light, texturing) while still making actors' faces visible.

2. *Defining place and space*: You can carve out any space you want on stage through lighting, and many shows do without sets almost entirely and rely on light to sculpt rooms, hallways, outdoor spaces— whatever is needed.

This can be extremely powerful both because of the variability of moods available in association with any space, and because scene changes can happen in- stantaneously (sometimes with the accompaniment of a sound cue), avoiding the need to move scenery or go to disruptive blackouts or brownouts, as in the work of lighting designer Andrea Lundy and others with Daniel MacIvor and Daniel Brooks.

3. *Achieving focus*: Light is a key way to get the audience to look at what you want them to. At its extreme this can mean hiding things on stage by leav- ing some parts of the stage in darkness while lighting others, but those extremes aren't always necessary. A difference in levels between one part of the stage and another, combined with strategic blocking, is usually enough.

It's also the case that moving light, which in- cludes the introduction of all but the subtlest light cue, draws the eye—think of fires, light on water, television screens in bars. An ill-chosen light cue, in fact, can often upstage the action if it's not used purposefully.

The brightest or lightest-coloured object on stage will attract the most light and therefore the most focus. If you want the audience to look at faces, they have to be the brightest thing on the stage—and when you're lighting Black actors or actors of colour, give them more light. Indeed, skin texture is always a factor: some actors just need more light than others.

Finally, even the lowest level of light on white or bright surfaces produces bounce and can defeat the most well-planned blackout.

4. *Creating atmosphere and mood*: Clearly light levels, intensities, angles, colours, and textures have everything to do with establishing or changing the mood of a scene, and this can be done either subtly or abruptly depending on the count of the cue.

5. *Providing information to audiences*: This happens in obvious ways—lighting can indicate time of day, weather, the arrival of a car at night, the switching on of a lamp or overhead interior light, the rising of the moon, the presence of fire, or the immanence of a storm.

But light can also play a role in telling the story in ways that are less obvious, particularly because of its capacity to reveal things that may hitherto have been unnoticed. As an obvious example (there are many more subtle ones), in a murder mystery, the central clue is often hiding in plain, underlit, sight.

6. *Supporting actors*: Light, like sound, can help actors by reinforcing the mood of a scene, underscoring an emotion, or providing a productive obstacle—such as the need to communicate when someone is shining a light into your eyes when you can't see her face.

7. *Shaping structure and rhythm, marking transitions*: This usually involves changing lighting states between acts, scenes, or other divisions, sometimes, but not necessarily, by using blackouts. Lighting changes (often accompanied by sound or music) can indicate passage of time, changes of place, and perhaps more importantly changes of mood.

Another consideration is the use of moving lights and follow spots, special effects, strobe lights, and disco balls. Again, moving light draws the eye and needs to be used very carefully. If well and selectively used, it can be very effective, and current technology allows a great deal to be done with moving lights cued from the lighting board. Moving lights, however, can be noisy, and should be avoided in small theatres and/or "covered" by sound cues.

Follow spots create an aura of theatricality, are often most useful in musicals or metatheatrical shows in large auditoria, and cost money for an operator's salary. Strobe lights should be used sparingly and disco balls should be avoided at all costs.

Projections

Projections of various kinds are more and more commonly used in live theatre, often not well, but equally often to brilliant effect. Projections should never be used for merely decorative or special effects purposes or as an inexpensive way to indicate time, place, and setting. They should be an integral part of the production throughout, functioning as an essential part of the vision, as one of the characters, part of the story, or central to what the production is about.

Focus is a major issue when it comes to projections: yet again, moving light draws the eye, and even without movement, projections tend to pull focus away from live action.

If you plan to use projections, one of the first considerations will be the source. For front projection you need to make sure that nothing, including actors, is blocking the surface onto which you're projecting. Rear projection can save a lot of trouble: rear projection screens usually produce a crisper image than front projection can, you don't have to worry about keystoning (angle distortion), and you don't have to worry about actors getting in the way of the beam.

Intensity is crucial. Projections only work if the light source is intense, and of course front lighting of the stage can easily wash out or render limp the crispest of projected images.

Another important consideration is the surfaces onto which you're projecting. To begin, you don't have to project onto screens. Often (in close consort with a set designer) projections can go all over a set, or be focused on specific panels or sheets (often most effectively when they are *not* flat), and on at least one occasion I've seen they can be tightly confined to actors' faces (or masks).

Be inventive. If you plan to use projections, you should use them boldly and without apology. You do, however, have to keep up with the technology. It's now possible and very effective to do projections "live," or to have them activated in a variety of ways by actors on the stage. If used carefully, live projections can even use and implicate the audience.

Smell, Touch, Taste

There are senses the theatre doesn't routinely appeal to, but in specific instances they can be used quite powerfully.

> *Smell* is the easiest, most often used atmospherically. The smell of food cooking in *Miss Julie*, for example, evokes the kitchen setting brilliantly (as food cooking often can); scents of flowers, incense, and so on, done subtly, can have hauntingly evocative impact because they tend to bypass consciousness.

> *Touch* between actors and audiences is generally too invasive or too intimate and can turn an audience member into a performer. But it can work in very specific cases, usually only by invitation. But even a handshake (or round of handshakes) can create a communal atmosphere (as in Ravi Jain and Asha Jain's *A Brimful of Asha*, where Ravi Jain welcomed

each audience member into the auditorium and intro-duced them to his mother), and handouts of leaflets or buttons can enhance a rally scene (if you avoid becoming precious). I've directed a show in which, representing the shutdown of a subversive perfor-mance, the audience was hustled out physically at the end by uniformed police, with no opportunity for curtain call or applause.

Other experiences of touch have to do with the textures of furnishings—an audience seated on the wooden rafters or hay bales of a barn in *The Farm Show* will experience the show very differently than one seated on plush velvet.

Taste is still more rare in the theatre, but shared food can evoke community, as when Bread and Puppet Theater in Vermont bakes and distributes bread at its performances, or when the audience is passed the hors d'oeuvres at an onstage dinner party, transform-ing them into guests. A recent production by Cahoots Theatre in Toronto, *A Taste of Empire*, was set in a demonstration kitchen and consisted of the prepa-ration of rellenong bangus, a traditional fish dish in the Philippines, while the chef/performer provided the colonial history and contemporary provenance of the ingredients. Audience members were offered servings of the completed dish at the end of the show.

14. TECH WEEK

I'm using the term tech week to refer to the period of time when all the elements of the show begin to come together. It doesn't always or usually involve a week, it doesn't only involve focusing on technical work (work with the cast should continue during this time), and in an ideal world technical elements—from sound to light to costumes, props, furniture, and work on the set will have been introduced earlier.

The stages of the work outlined here are not always separate and may take different amounts of time depending on the technical demands and complexities of the show. Nevertheless, a typical rehearsal period will draw toward its close as the company moves from the rehearsal hall onto the set and into the theatre (an Equity day off for actors is usually set aside for a *load in*), after which there will be, sometimes concurrently, some version of each of the following elements: a *paper tech*, *hang and focus*, *level set*, *cue to cue*, *tech run*, sometimes a *costume parade*, a *tech dress*, one or more *dress rehearsals*, a *preview* or previews, and an *opening night* (or "press night"). These need to be scheduled carefully and realistically, and if you don't feel enough time has been scheduled for any part of this you need to argue for more.

This period can be fraught:

1. Actors are beginning to go public, but much of the focus of the work is not on them and they can spend a great deal of time feeling bored or miffed;

2. Control of the show is beginning to shift away from the director to stage management; and

3. Technicians are just beginning their work when there usually isn't much time left in the process and everyone else is feeling impatient with them.

The best thing you can bring to this period as a director is patience, good humour, and the capacity to relax and make everyone else feel relaxed. The last thing anybody needs is a nervous or stroppy director.

At the same time you have to develop the capacity to concentrate closely on what's going on and to see and hear clearly, keeping the needs of the show as a whole in mind.

Protocol is important during tech week. It has both to be made clear and be clearly followed, and this is normally the provenance of the stage manager, but you should make sure that it's done.

The stage manager is responsible for running tech and should be in touch with all departments (sets, sound, lights, costumes), the dressing room, and the green room over headsets, as well as with backstage crew—including usually an *assistant stage manager* (ASM) or ASMs in charge of costumes and props.

The stage manager records in the prompt book where all standbys and cues are called (figure 12); board operators

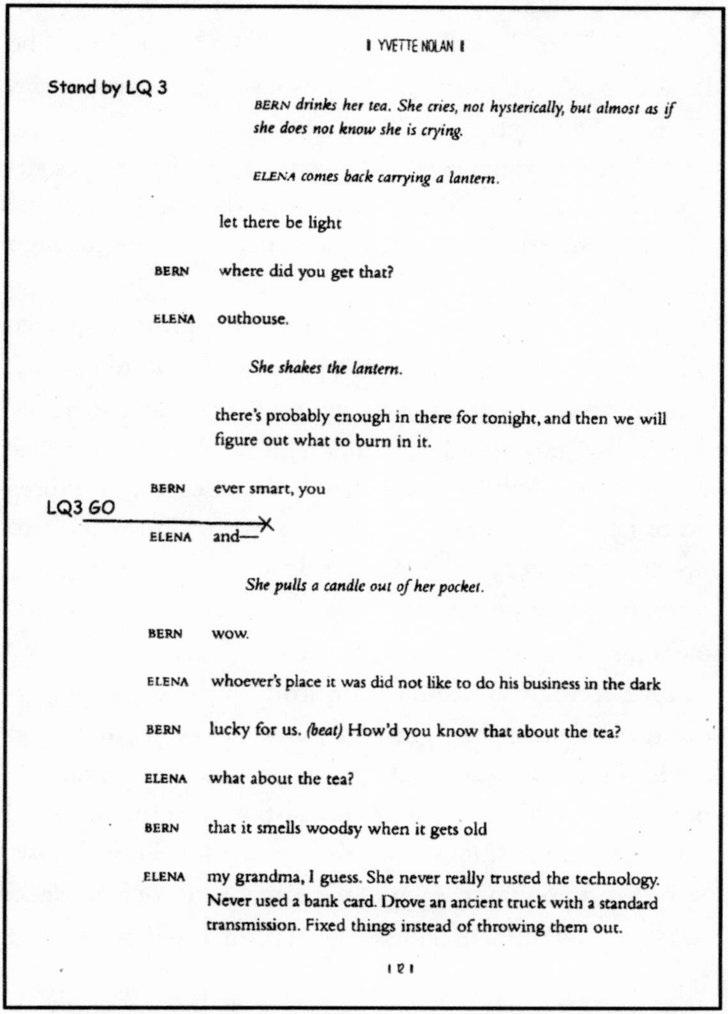

Stand by LQ 3

BERN drinks her tea. She cries, not hysterically, but almost as if she does not know she is crying.

ELENA comes back carrying a lantern.

let there be light

BERN   where did you get that?

ELENA   outhouse.

She shakes the lantern.

there's probably enough in there for tonight, and then we will figure out what to burn in it.

BERN   ever smart, you

LQ3 GO ——————————✕

ELENA   and—

She pulls a candle out of her pocket.

BERN   wow.

ELENA   whoever's place it was did not like to do his business in the dark

BERN   lucky for us. *(beat)* How'd you know that about the tea?

ELENA   what about the tea?

BERN   that it smells woodsy when it gets old

ELENA   my grandma, I guess. She never really trusted the technology. Never used a bank card. Drove an ancient truck with a standard transmission. Fixed things instead of throwing them out.

161

Figure 12: Mock-up of a page from a prompt book for Yvette Nolan's *The Unplugging*.

record precisely what the cues consist of. As tech proceeds the stage manager will call standbys ("standby LQ 7") and cues ("LQ 7: go"), and no one else in the theatre should be allowed to use the word "go" unless it's an actor speaking a line from the script.

As director you'll need to be consulting with the designers throughout about the nature of the cues and costumes, but communication with the board operators goes through the stage manager.

The theatre during tech can often be a bit messy, since building has either just been completed or is still underway. Nevertheless, enough aisles have to be kept clear to allow you, the assistant director, and designers to roam the house in order to see lighting states from all angles and distances and to hear the sound from all parts of the house. It's also important to keep the air free of dust (especially sawdust) by frequent mopping or spraying. Dust can destroy actors' voices just when they need them most.

As director you should sit in front of the stage manager and in front of the light and sound desks, the lights on which can inhibit seeing lighting states accurately. Either on your own or with the help of an assistant director you need to make sure that things work from every seat in the house.

It's worth outlining each of the components of tech week, though not all of them necessarily happen as distinct events:

1. A *paper tech* isn't always done and may not be necessary. Often, however, it's a good idea either as part of a production meeting or in a separate meeting to sit down with the stage manager and the sound

and lighting designers at the beginning of tech week to talk through the script, marking in pencil in the prompt copy where anticipated sound and light cues will be called and what those cues will consist of. Some of these will have been recorded throughout the rehearsal process, but this record is rarely complete and often inaccurate. A paper tech can save a great deal of time later and can help to make sure that everyone is on the same page.

2. Before *level set* the lighting crew will have completed a preliminary *hang and focus* from the lighting plot, speakers will have been positioned, and sounds created or collected, all in consultation with you as necessary.

The level set that follows involves sitting in the theatre, seeing all light states and cues sequentially, hearing all sound cues, adjusting as necessary, and setting levels and the approximate counts on which they'll come in.

It's usually best to work through the show setting both light and sound cues as they occur rather than working through the show once for sound and once for lights. Light and sound cues often coincide and counts usually have to be synchronized.

Normally actors aren't called for level set (they usually find it tedious and probably have better things to do, and lighting designers often find the presence of actors annoying and distracting). But walkers are needed to stand in for them and walk through light states as you and the designer assess levels and check for dips and hot spots. Walkers should be asked to wear dark colours or colours that approximate those of the costumes, and if at all possible walkers should have skin colours that approximate those of the actors.

As director you need to keep focused on what you're seeing and hearing and on how it supports or fails to support the show. You need to discuss with the designers what changes or adjustments need to be made to the cues, trying to avoid telling them how to do their jobs. It's better to indicate what you'd like to see and hear than to indicate how to do it.

The level set should be moved through efficiently, but be sure to take enough time to check each cue thoroughly, particularly to make sure that all parts of the stage have the light levels that you need where you need them.

When setting sound levels, remember that you're in an empty auditorium and that levels will feel lower when it's filled with bodies (and in winter in Canada, coats).

3. Many productions, particularly in smaller theatres and particularly where there are a lot of cues, now incorporate a *cue-to-cue* into the tech run, but it's important to understand it as a separate function in order to remain focused on the work it contributes.

The cue-to-cue involves focusing on and moving through each cue in the show, beginning just before the standby is called and stopping just after the cue is complete. The cast has to be called for the cue-to-cue, and they have to operate at something close to performance level since the timing of each cue (its calling and its count) must be coordinated with their lines and movements.

If the level set has been thoroughly and carefully done cue-to-cue will only involve minor adjustments to levels and counts, but there always are such adjustments.

If there are major changes that involve rehanging instruments, moving speakers, or finding or creating new sounds, these are best handled through notes, with the changes being made afterward.

This is a difficult rehearsal for a director. You have to be responsive and attentive to the tech as well as the actors, and the actors often get restless.

The end of cue-to-cue, if there's time, is often the best time to block the *curtain call*: the crew is there, levels are being set, and plotting the curtain call can end a difficult night on a cheerful or even celebratory note. Curtain calls involve the actors graciously accepting applause on behalf of the company and allowing the audience to have their say. They should be neither self-indulgently lengthy nor ungraciously foreclosed. They should be blocked as carefully as any scene in the show and should feature the cast in attractive and welcoming ways.

4. The *tech run* is an uninterrupted run-through of the show unless there are serious issues, particularly around safety, that would merit disrupting it.

While the focus of the tech run is on tech, and as director you need to be paying full attention to and taking notes on the ways in which tech is shaping the show's overall rhythms, moods, and sequencings, it's also important that the actors feel the full impact of the tech on their performances for the first time, and they will also need some attention.

Make sure that plenty of time is scheduled after the tech run for tech notes. It may be necessary to give actors their notes by email because of time constraints, but notes in person are better if you can manage it.

5. The *tech dress* is the first run of the show with both costumes and tech. There may have been a *costume parade* scheduled some time before the tech dress to give yourself, the designers, and costume crew the chance to see and adjust all of the costumes and combinations of costumes on the actors and under their lights—but often there isn't time for this or it's not necessary.

Before the tech dress the costume crew and ASM in charge of costumes will have tracked where and how costume changes occur, how costumes and props travel backstage to where they're needed, and how any quick changes are to be accomplished. Part of the purpose of the tech dress is to make sure this plotting is working properly.

Make sure that lots of time is scheduled for the actors to get into costume and makeup: this is also usually the first opportunity to see makeup under the lights.

The tech dress, again, should be an uninterrupted run of the show followed by notes. The focus this time is on both tech and costumes—or more specifically on the relationship between the two. How do the costumes look and operate under the lights and in relation to everything else? Are unanticipated changes in level, direction, or coverage needed? Do the calls or counts need adjustments because the use of costumes has introduced unanticipated delays? Are adjustments to the costumes themselves necessary in order for a quick change to be completed in time (cutting an accessory, adding Velcro, etc.)? Is an extra dresser necessary in the wings? (Note, though, that quick changes get quicker and more comfortable as actors and dressers get used to doing them.) Do the costumes make unanticipated noise that disrupts or disguises the soundscape? Are adjustments to the makeup necessary?

This run can be a difficult one for actors who have become comfortable in their rehearsal clothes and are working with the actual costumes and makeup for the first time, so don't be surprised if the show doesn't seem up to its usual snuff.

Again, make sure that plenty of time is scheduled after the tech dress for costume and tech notes. And again, it may be necessary to give actors their notes by email because of time constraints, but notes in person are better if you can manage it.

6. *Dress rehearsals* should be uninterrupted runs of the full show, observing pre-show, intermission, and post-show timing, calls, and protocols, sometimes to an invited audience whose judgment and good will you trust. Dress rehearsals exist for a few reasons:

a) To let the actors get comfortable with the tech and costumes and return to the centre of focus;

b) To allow you to identify parts of the show that need work and to schedule rehearsals to work on them;

c) To make final adjustments to light, sound, and costume elements; and

d) To invite feedback from trusted outsiders (these will often include the theatre's artistic director and/or the show's producers).

7. *Previews* are performances before a paying audience (usually at reduced prices) that precede the opening. They provide you with the chance to see the show through the audience's eyes. It's astonishing how different a show can feel under these circumstances and how often directors sit through previews thinking, "Why on earth did I make *that* choice!"

Previews provide the last chance to make changes or to go back (briefly) into rehearsal and fix or enrich things. The first preview will also be the first real test of sound levels with an audience in the house, so pay close attention to them and adjust accordingly.

Don't hesitate to make other changes that have to be made for the sake of the show's integrity or clarity. It's crucial to make sure that the audience is actually following what they need to follow. Be sensitive to any places where it feels as though you're losing them, and be willing to restage or even cut sequences.

But don't be a feather for each wind that blows: lack of laughter at a given point, for example, doesn't mean the moment isn't working or that the next night's audience won't laugh.

8. For many directors *opening night* (or morning, or afternoon, in the case of school shows) is the last chance to see the show before leaving it in the hands of the stage manager, who will, however, send show reports.

Rarely is there the opportunity to go back into rehearsal once a show has opened. Some actors even resent receiving notes from the director after opening, but this is silly: a good actor will welcome necessary or helpful notes at any time.

9. You'll continue to get *show reports* from stage management after every performance. Most of the time these can be received simply for information, trusting the stage manager, who at this point is in charge, to make sure that the show maintains its form and to deal with any deviations or discrepancies.

If your stage manager asks for or seems to need help in dealing with something, you should of course make yourself available for consultation, advice, and suggestions. In extreme cases, if union contracts and budgets permit, emergency rehearsals can be called to fix things that have gone seriously wrong, or to rehearse with a replacement cast member, but such occasions are fortunately rare.

15. CONCLUSION

This book has been intended as a practical guide to fundamentals only. Beyond insisting on the director's having or finding a personal or social need to stage a production, it has spent little time on the director as an artist or on the theatre as an art form, and it's only briefly mentioned a director's "vision," which is, of course, crucial, and which is what makes the difference between a competent production and an important or brilliant one.

The book has made two assumptions: that brilliance without competence is wasted, and that artistic vision is something that develops over time and through accumulated experience, in the art form and in the world.

That experience, however, can be prepared for and shaped, so I want to end with some general suggestions—beyond getting as much training as possible in as many kinds of theatre as possible—about how an aspiring director might usefully prepare. To this end I've assembled ten tips adapted and expanded from a list by British director John Caird:

1. *Read promiscuously.* Read plays, novels, poetry, adaptations, screenplays, histories, biographies, diaries, sociology, psychology, science, theory, and criticism. Read theatre journals, magazines, and blogs. And read

everything about the plays, playwrights, and theatre companies that most interest you.

2. *Go to galleries, exhibitions, and installations*. A large part of directing is developing a strong visual sensibility, and part of this has to do with familiarizing yourself with historical and contemporary art from a wide range of cultures and periods, including painting, sculpture, performance art, installations, architecture, and collage—particularly work that occupies three dimensions.

3. *Listen to music*. All kinds of music, from all periods and places. Another central component of directing is aural, melodic, and rhythmic, and knowledge of a musical repertoire will help enormously in talking with designers and composers.

4. *Go to the theatre*. All sorts of theatre. Whatever you can afford—and if you can't afford it, volunteer to usher or help out, anything that gets you in the door. See everything you can. Don't be overly discriminating, but do try to follow closely the kinds of work that most interest you, track the work of directors and companies whose work you admire, and try to be as clear as possible in your own mind about what it is you like about them.

5. *Travel*. There's theatre all over the world. Broaden your view about what constitutes good theatre and

performance by seeing it in as many traditions and cultures as possible, and if you can't afford to travel, watch films, DVDs and YouTube. If you speak another language, don't let it slide. Practise it, study its theatre. Broaden your mind and your experience.

6. *Meet playwrights and actors.* Playwrights are among the primary creative forces in theatre. Get to know them. Read their plays. Help them develop their work if you can. Set up readings with actors.

Directors should love actors. If you don't look forward to the time you spend with actors and genuinely appreciate actors' processes, you probably should reconsider whether you want to direct. Actors are remarkable: what they do, in rehearsal and in performance, is astonishing. Study it. Try to understand the creative chemistry of actors at work and try to get to know as many different ways of communicating with actors as possible.

7. *Assemble a group of like-minded people and produce shows.* No matter how small in scale or low in budget. Try early on to get into fringe festivals and venues with projects you're passionate about. Learn from your successes or failures and move on.

8. *Work as an assistant.* Write to all directors whose work you admire. Explain why you think you should work with them. If you get taken on, pay attention—be a sponge. Learn everything you can about how people

you admire work, but don't attempt simply to mimic them, and don't get addicted to assisting or let it become an excuse for not doing your own work.

9. *Work in the theatre.* Any temporary job will help, in as many aspects of theatre as possible. Directors should understand how every aspect of theatre works, in rehearsal and in production. Get a job in the wardrobe department, with the stage crew, or in the lighting or sound departments, as a dramaturge, an actor, an administrator, or a publicist. The more you know, and the more you know about what *all* the people who work in the theatre do, the better director you'll be. But don't get stuck as a would-be director in a full-time job as an administrator or publicist. Volunteer, take contract work, and keep your options open.

10. *Observe the world.* Learn to closely observe people, behaviour, situations, social structures and organizations, business, family, politics, law, sports, celebrity and popular culture, marginalized subcultures, people from cultures other than your own. Pay attention. Analyze each of these accurately: what structural, psychological, social, cultural, and historical pressures are at play?*

This book is intended as a beginning; the rest is up to you.

---

* This list draws directly upon, but expands and (mis)quotes, Caird's "Want to be a theatre director? Here are my 10 top survival tips," http://www.guardian.co.uk/stage/theatreblog/2010/mar/23/theatre-director-10-top-tips.

APPENDIX A:
NEW PLAY DEVELOPMENT

Sooner or later in Canada most directors end up working on new plays. This is a privilege, and the responsibility that comes with it shouldn't be taken lightly. If you're lucky and there's a budget for it, it's best to work with an experienced dramaturge. If not this appendix is intended to give you some sense of the kinds of questions you might want to ask the writers of new work and what kind of processes of new play development you might find yourself engaged in.

Dramaturgical Questions*

It's sometimes difficult to know how to respond to a new play that comes across your desk, either directly from the playwright or from a theatre company inviting you to direct it. The questions that follow are intended to offer a starting point for thinking about new work. They relate directly to those asked by a director doing a script analysis of any play (see Section One), but they're framed to help you support

---

* This questionnaire is an expanded and modified version of an unpublished one developed by playwright, director, actor, and dramaturge Guillermo Verdecchia.

playwrights in deciding how close what they've written comes to what they wanted to write.

These questions aren't intended to be a template or universal model, and not all of the questions will be appropriate to all plays. Crucially, they should be adapted, with some jettisoned and some expanded upon, depending on the play and playwright you're working with. They begin with general questions about story, plot, action, and structure; follow with questions about character, dialogue, and mode; and end with questions about individual scenes.

1. *General (subject, story, plot, action, and structure)*

a) What's the play about? State it very briefly (e.g., *Hamlet* is about revenge).

b) Why should the audience care? Does the play assume that the audience already cares about the subject, or does it successfully *make* them care? What engages them?

c) What *happens*? What is the story, if there is one? As an exercise, try to tell it chronologically from beginning to end, preferably in a single sentence or *short* paragraph. If there is no story, what's the *action* that's performed?

d) Whose story is it (what individual, group, community, or collectivity)?

e) How does the story relate to the *plot*? Does it unfold chronologically? Does it begin *in medias res* (in the middle of things)? At the end? Does it involve flashbacks? Why? If there is backstory, how is it revealed? If there are one or more supporting subplots, how do they relate to the main plot? Are they necessary? As an exercise, chart the plot in relation to the story.

f) What does the central character, group, community, or collective want? How strongly (how high are the stakes)? As a general rule, the higher the stakes, the more compelling the play is.

g) What's stopping her, him, or them? How significant are the obstacles (how high are the stakes)? As a general rule, again, the higher the stakes, the more compelling the play is.

h) What event or decision initiates the action? Who or what does this initiating? How directly and with what impact does this introduce what the play is about and why it matters? How does this initiating event hook the audience?

i) What forces or characters drive the action throughout?

j) What changes through the course of the play?

k) At what precise moments do things change? At what points in the play are new complications, reversals, false resolutions, and resolutions introduced? What's the shape of the play? As an exercise, chart the play on a scene-by-scene or unit-by-unit graph, marking precisely where significant changes happen. How does the play start, how does it end, and how does it get there?

l) What's *necessary* to do what the play wants to do? Is every element, every character, every scene needed? Why? Is there flab? Are there extra characters? Extra details? Is there self-indulgence?

m) What's the *world* of the play? By what rules, laws, or conventions does it operate? Are these conventions established clearly? What's the relationship between that world and the "real world"? Are the rules of the play world consistently adhered to or productively broken? (These questions are particularly acute in expressionist, impressionist, or absurdist plays, or plays that invoke any kind of supernatural or magical elements.)

n) Are the connections among scenes, events, stories, actions, and characters clear? If they are unclear, or hidden, or their revelation is delayed is there a good reason for this?

o) What spaces and places does the action occur in? Are they fixed? How do they relate to one another? Are there too many to keep clear? To be reasonably staged? How are events that happen outside of those spaces represented? Are they represented consistently?

p) What's the time frame of the action? What's the duration of the represented action's "present tense" (i.e., does the action take place in "real time," over a few days, a week, a year, a lifetime)? How is the temporality represented, and how does it relate to the real time of the audience watching the play? What temporal "slice" of the story is the audience watching? How is what happens outside of that time frame represented and is it represented consistently? If not, why not? Are the inconsistencies productive?

q) How many characters are in each scene? Does this vary from scene to scene, or become static? Does something new happen when another character enters a scene (or when a new scene begins)?

r) What's the rhythm of the play? Are there slower, more regular moments? Quicker, more jagged ones? Does the rhythm become predictable? Are all the scenes the same length? Are there rhythmic surprises? To what effect?

s) What's the music of the play? Are there dissonances that resolve into harmonies? Dissonances that aren't resolved? Is this productive? Are the resolutions achieved too easily? Are those things left unresolved productive (or just cop-outs)? Are the scenes all in the same key?

2. *Characters/Roles*

a) What forces does each character bring into the play and what pressures do they put on one another? (Think of the characters as forces, vectors, dramatic postulates, or "what if" propositions).

b) How does each character speak? Think of *diction* (what worlds, classes, or discourses the words come from), *imagery* (what worlds their figurative language derives from), *syntax* (how they put their sentences together), *rhythm* (the flow of their speech, its regularity or irregularity, its tempo, its pace), and *grammar* (proper or colloquial). Are the characters' ways of speaking distinct from one another? Are they consistent with the stories and backstories of the characters, their social positionings? Are they consistent with the characters' actions (and if not is this a productive difference)?

c) What does each character say about herself? What is said about her character by others? Are these consistent or revealingly inconsistent? Are they consistent with what she *does*?

3. *Dialogue*

a) Is the dialogue crisp, clean, witty? Languorous, relaxed, verbose? Is this appropriate to the subject, the story, the relationships between the characters speaking?

b) Is the pacing varied?

c) Does each line *do* something (as opposed to simply describing or telling something)? Is the language *active*? Even when a line is there to provide backstory, it *also* has to perform some action in the moment and have an impact on the other characters and/or the audience.

4. *Mode*

a) Are there narrative, lyrical, and dramatic moments in the play? Are the shifts between these modes productive or awkward?

b) If there are moments of narrative (in which characters *tell* stories), do they interrupt the action productively? Do they also *do* something (have an impact on the other characters, on the audience)?

c) If there are lyrical moments (of pure description or expression) do they interrupt the action productively? Do they also *do* something (have an impact on the other characters, on the audience)?

d) In most theatre the dramatic mode predominates: stories are *shown* rather than told. If this is not the case in this play, are there good and productive reasons for this? In each case would it be stronger to show rather than tell? Why not?

5. *Individual scenes (or units)*

a) What does the scene (or unit) accomplish? Advance the plot? Complicate the action? Increase the stakes? Reveal character?

Develop the theme? A good scene does several of these things. A great scene does all of them.

b) What does the audience know at the end of the scene/unit that they didn't know at the beginning and how is this accomplished?

c) Does the scene/unit build in some coherent way on the one that precedes it and lead coherently to the one that follows?

d) Is it clear what each character or force in the scene or unit is pushing for (or against)?

e) Is there flab or self-indulgence?

f) Has all the information been provided—about the characters, the situation, the stakes—in order for the audience to understand the scene? Has too much information been provided, leaving the scene repetitious or boring and leaving nothing for the audience to work out for themselves?

g) How does the scene relate to the larger story or action? Does it move them forward? Is the information in the scene coming at the right moment in the play? Should it come earlier? Later? Does it need to come at all?

h) Is the scene or unit complete in itself?

i) Does the scene (apart from the play's final scene) leave the audience prematurely satisfied, with all tension resolved, or does it leave them wanting (to know) more?

j) Is it engaging and worth watching in itself? What, for the audience, is the "hook"? What should they care about? What engages them?

Don't ask the playwright these questions in your first meeting, or all at once, and when you do ask some version of some of them, modify and tailor the questions to the specifics of the play you're working on and the readiness of the playwright to hear them.

Process

Play development processes can vary significantly, depending on the point at which you and all concerned feel the play is ready to go into rehearsal. What follows is an account of a typical process in theatres in Canada that deal with new play development funded through the Canada Council for the Arts and/or other regional funding bodies.

1. *First meeting*

You'll have read the latest draft of the play before your first meeting with the playwright, but that shouldn't be the main focus of the meeting, which should ideally be simply about getting to know one another. It is often best to meet over a meal, a drink, or some other informal but private occasion.

You should ask questions: what is her or his background, what does s/he care about, what compelled her or him to write, what kinds of things does s/he find interesting, what films/music/books/artists does s/he like, and so on. In this meeting you shouldn't, as director/dramaturge, do most of the talking, but should focus on listening, on getting a sense of the writer and her or his priorities and ways of thinking.

Either late in the first meeting or (better) in a subsequent meeting it's good to start asking the writer to articulate in a simple sentence or two what the play is about and why it matters. This is something to hang on to and return to as the development process proceeds and the writer gets input from all quarters. You may well find it useful later on to say, "You said in June that the play was about X, is that still the case?"

You'll probably have several meetings after the first one and before the first, "phase one" workshop. These are best used, first, for asking some of the questions I've outlined above, as appropriate, and second, for telling the playwright what *you* get from the play.

You should try not to make suggestions at this stage, but ask questions about anything that isn't clear to you (about plot, characters, language—anything). This lets the writer know that you haven't understood something, but doesn't tell her or him that, or how, it needs to be clarified—s/he may not want it understood, or may not feel that it's necessary to clarify, or may choose to clarify in ways that you haven't anticipated. The playwright will know that you haven't understood and at this stage can deal with that information as and if s/he wants to.

Telling the playwright what you understand the play to be about and what you think it's doing, followed by the question "Is that what you wanted the audience to get?" is also much better than making suggestions. You serve at this stage as a kind of surrogate audience.

2. *First workshop*

In Canada a first workshop is usually four or eight hours, with actors, director/dramaturge, a stage manager/administrator, and occasionally (if called for by the nature of the project) a movement person, ideally a designer, or whoever is necessary.

Workshops are best cast with actors who are good at doing workshops rather than actors that you may want to cast eventually for the roles—though these may be the same people. But don't let the actors use a workshop to audition for the part, to show off, or to fight for the importance of their character (and therefore the size of their role). The purpose of a workshop is to serve the development of the play.

After introductions are made and people settle in, the playwright may want to introduce the script before the workshop begins, giving the actors any information they need about the setting, the characters, pronunciations, situations, or indeed the reason for writing the play. Otherwise, the first workshop usually starts with a reading.

The main purpose of the read-through is to give the playwright (and also you, as director/dramaturge) a chance to hear the play. The cast should have received the script and been assigned their roles a couple of days in advance and will usually have done some preparation.

Someone other than the playwright or yourself should be assigned to read the stage directions.

Following the read-through there is usually a controlled discussion—controlled because playwright and play at this stage are fragile and the playwright sometimes overly suggestible. Don't let the actors criticize the script or make suggestions about how it should be rewritten or staged. A good way of starting is to ask everyone in the room to indicate what they most liked about the script, what they found most compelling, or what image they found most striking.

This can usefully be followed by asking the actors to ask the playwright questions about the characters they're playing, things that aren't clear to them or that they don't understand. Don't let them ask broader questions, and do make clear to the playwright that, while s/he should take notes, s/he doesn't *have* to answer any question unless s/he wants to.

Usually after the read-through it's good to meet privately with the playwright to talk about her or his reactions to it and to the questions that have come up, and plan a way forward. You may need to be vigilant about making sure the playwright doesn't change the play because an actor or actors read particularly well or badly. A bad reading doesn't mean the writing isn't working, and a particularly good one may just mean that the actor is good at making almost anything come alive. Even at this early stage, your dramaturgical role is to protect the play, even, if necessary, from the playwright.

If you have eight hours rather than four, it's best to take the second four hours on a second day, allowing the playwright to do rewrites in between, and then to do another reading the next day with a similar procedure.

3. *Second workshop*

A second workshop is held after significant revisions have been done—sometimes as much as a year after the first, during which time you or your dramaturge will have worked with the playwright one-on-one and perhaps worked through more of the dramaturgical questions I've listed above, as appropriate.

The second workshop is usually longer than the first one—a couple of days, a weekend, sometimes even a week or more—and if at all possible it should involve a designer or designers.

The second workshop is different from the first in that it's usually beginning to imagine staging possibilities, design possibilities, movement, and so on. It begins with a reading, but then works through the play a scene at a time, and it usually ends with a public presentation of some kind—often a staged reading. This allows the playwright to get a better sense of the relationships among the characters and between the characters and the space. It allows her or him—and you, as director—to get a sense of what does or doesn't work in front of an audience, especially what scenes or moments might be too long, too complicated, or too perfunctory.

The public presentation also allows for feedback in some form or other from the audience. It's essential, especially with new or emerging artists, to protect the playwright from this feedback. I tend to ask for any feedback to come to me in writing rather than in a talkback, and I filter it so that the playwright doesn't ever read anything that might be damaging or hurtful, or might cause her or him to change the play in unfortunate ways. I pass on comments that tell the playwright what an audience member might have seen, understood, or misunderstood during the reading.

Further work will take place between you, the dramaturge, and the playwright before the play goes into rehearsal, and there may be more workshops. But eventually, unless the project is abandoned, the show at this stage will be scheduled for production.

4. *Rehearsal and production*

It's best once the show goes into rehearsal that there be a production dramaturge who is not the director, but whose job it is to continue to work with the playwright on script changes and also on the dramaturgy and shape of the performance itself and with the actors on their research. The production dramaturge tries to keep the playwright's intentions in mind, making sure that they aren't distorted, and again protects the play from you as director, the actors, and the playwright her/himself, who is often overly eager to accommodate requests that may or may not be in the play's best interests.

As director you need to be careful not to let your vision for the play ride roughshod over that of the playwright, and you need to work in close co-operation with the production dramaturge throughout the process. Where possible, however, you may want to resist making major script changes at a late stage, which can disorient the actors.

APPENDIX B: DEVISING

Not all directing projects involve working with scripts. Increasingly, directors are involved in collective or collaborative projects that start from scratch, and text, if there is any, evolves alongside all other elements of a production.

Devised projects are infinitely various, but they usually begin with a group of artists who share an urgent interest in an initial question or idea. Devised projects also tend to share some essential features, including a refusal of primacy to text, a shift of priorities from product to process, a heightened engagement with space and place, an exploration of emergent technologies, and a fundamental interdisciplinarity. Canadian director, dramaturge, playwright, and scholar Bruce Barton argues that these principles underlie a distinctive approach to composition in devised work, which tends to rely on improvisation, multiple authorship, found and adapted text, physical gesture, and structural principles such as collage, montage, "con-fusion," weaving, or quilting.[*]

---

[*]   Bruce Barton, "Devising the Creative Body," introduction to *Collective Creation, Collaboration, and Devising* (Toronto: Playwrights Canada, 2008), xix.

As a director, particularly in the early stages of a devising project, your role will be fundamentally generative and dramaturgical.

Geoffrey Proehl identifies dramaturgy as "the name given to that set of elements necessary to the working of a play at any moment in its passage from imagination to embodiment," and he identifies those elements as "its *repetitions and patterns*," "its unfolding *narratives*," "its unique *world*," "its *characters*," "its *spectacles*," its "*metatheatre*," and its literary, organic, and spatial "*structures*." *

These elements generally characterize both scripted and devised work, but they are particularly apt as guideposts to structuring the dramaturgical analysis of devised work as it passes "from imagination to embodiment." It's not necessary always to address each element separately or to address all of them, but they work well as a checklist.

I'll begin here, however, with the question, idea, and the *urgency* that drive the project.

---

* Geoffrey S. Proehl, with DD Kugler, Mark Lamos, and Michael Lupu, *Toward a Dramaturgical Sensibility: Landscape and Journey* (Cranberry, NJ: Associated University Presses, 2008), 19–20, emphasis added.

Urgency

The dramaturgical analysis that subtends all devising projects is driven by an idea or question that's urgent for the creators and this question has to be foregrounded throughout. There are instances, especially in postmodern productions, in which devisers claim that their inspirations are random, derived from arbitrarily or accidentally assembled resources. I would argue that while this may be true, the arbitrariness of the selection process masks an urgency that may not, at least in the initial exploratory stages of the work, have risen to the level of consciousness.

A good first step for a director/dramaturge working on a devised project is to help the company identify what it is they want to know, what their devising efforts are directed at uncovering, and why. Devising, at its best, is research into something that's understood by the creators to be urgent. Devising projects that are developed out of a fabricated need often seem like exercises in cleverness for its own sake.

Methodology

In any devised production, the identification of a research question must be followed by a methodology by which to go about answering that question: a sense of how to proceed. This usually means identifying, finding, collecting, or inventing the resources needed to answer the question, and identifying or inventing a process by which those resources can be brought together, mined, manipulated, deconstructed, reassembled, sequenced, and given a structure.

Resources

The first and perhaps most important of the assembled resources for a show is the personnel. In devising, this is at once more crucial and less obvious than when you're working with a script, in that the roles are less predetermined.

Yes, you'll probably need someone to play the roles of director, designers, and performers at the very least, but what kinds of designers, and how many performers, of what background, training, gender, age, ethnicity, or other social signifiers? Does the project require a writer? A designated researcher or consultant on its subject matter? Does it call for, say, a videographer? Dancers, clowns, aerialists, or people with other specialized training? Someone who can paint or sculpt live or live-on-screen during the performance? In short, is there a particular range of expertise that's required to respond fully or usefully to the question that drives the process?

Perhaps more importantly, is everyone equally committed to that question? No matter how skilled a contributor to a devised process is, if she's not fully committed to the project, she won't pull her weight as a co-creator.

Other resources can include almost anything that's useful to addressing the project's central research question. These can include objects, images, photographs, paintings, poems, songs, music, stories, interviews, newspaper clippings, histories, biographies, documentaries, memories, YouTube clips, places, spaces, materials, textures, colours, dances, rituals, fragments of performance, genealogies, plants, flowers, scents, tastes, bodies, skills, or the company's own biographies, opinions, and perspectives.

The research or gathering phase of devised work can be endless and omnivorous and the relevance of the material introduced by members of the team may not be immediately clear to all concerned. This is usually a good thing, as it provides a starting point for explorations. This phase does not, of course, take place in isolation from the rest of the process, and new resources can be introduced at any time they seem necessary to fill a gap, solve a problem, or extend an exploration.

Even the richest assemblage of personnel and other resources, however, requires dramaturgical analysis from the outset in order to unlock their potential and orchestrate them formally as the basis of an evolving process. This analysis often devolves upon the director, who inevitably plays a dramaturgical role, whether or not this role is carried out in consort with an officially designated dramaturge.

Process

A key part of the dramaturgical and analytical work on any devised project is on the design of the process itself: any work of art—and this is particularly true of performance—can be understood to be a record or representation of its creation process.

Designing a devising process involves a kind of orchestration: *how* does the collective address and animate the assembled materials, what patterns and relationships does it perceive among them, what narratives, characters, forces, worlds, images, and spectacles are incipient in them, and how can the group work toward their physicalization and organization into a performance that addresses the questions it's set out to ask?

Throughout most devising processes, it's best to consider almost everyone in the room to be a "performer," and in all cases this should include musicians, designers, videographers, and others whose work needs to interact with all other aspects of the show as it evolves. In what follows I intend phrases such as "the group," "the performers," "the actors," and "improvisers" to include in particular those working on music, lights, sound, video, and projections as well as performers and perhaps others.

Most devising processes benefit from being structured as a series of creation workshops with enough time between each to conduct new research and undertake the analysis of what was accomplished in the previous one(s). And most devising processes consist of three overlapping phases: *analysis and embodiment* (of resources), *improvisation and annotation*, and *structuring*.

1. *Analysis and embodiment*

The first step is usually to address analytically what the members of the creative team have brought to the project, both individually and as a collective: the initial question, quite literally, is "*What* are *we* all doing *here*?" with each element of the question—the group, the activity, and the place and time—receiving equal attention.

It's usually up to you as director/dramaturge to answer this by coming up with something productive for us all to do.

The second, related question is "What are these artifacts and other resources doing here, what do they consist of, and what pressures do they bring to bear on our central question(s)?" Again, it's usually up to you as director/dramaturge to undertake—or, better, to orchestrate—this analysis.

Some directors will start with a kind of table work, initiating group analysis of the assembled materials and their relationship to the project. This has the advantage of involving everyone, including non-performers, from the outset, and establishing an analytical ground from which to build.

Others will begin by asking the collective to work as a group with their own bodies in motion, exploring the space and mining themselves and their relationships as resources before eventually introducing other materials—objects, poems, songs, fragments of story, and so on.

Others still will start by assigning specific resources to individual performers, asking them to devise improvisations in response to one, or a particular combination, of the gathered materials, either choosing ones that they have themselves introduced to the group, or deliberately selecting ones that they haven't and are therefore able to respond to spontaneously. Once each performer has presented one or more "turns," monologues, improvs, or items, the director begins to tease out patterns, connections, and themes, and to bring the performers together.

At this early stage there shouldn't be any pressure on the performers to craft the material into scenes, to take narrative or thematic coherence into account, or to consider audiences. This phase is best understood to consist of creating relationships and animating materials.

As director, you'll find your own ways of moving from the initially assembled team and materials through their analysis to the early stages of embodiment, always depending in specific ways on the topic under exploration, the team, and the space you're working with. There will be an element of exploration in this each time, but this shouldn't be either arbitrary or peremptory on the part of a director.

2. *Improvisation and annotation*

Once the first stages of exploration are over there are any number of ways of working, but most of them involve creating units of action that can eventually be structured dramaturgically into a show. Most directors develop individual units through the use of group improvisation around the fragments and interactions that have emerged from the first stage.

These improvisations should never be random or arbitrary, nor should they be selected or shaped simply on the basis of what is emerging that is most theatrical or most immediately entertaining, moving, or powerful in themselves. These questions of theatrical efficacy shouldn't be ignored, of course, but at this stage in particular improvisations should always be directed toward mining the work that is underway to uncover or illuminate some aspect of the larger question that drives the project and gives it its purpose.

If an improvisation seems at all useful it should be given time to develop. Often an improvisation doesn't hit its stride for ten, fifteen, twenty minutes or more. Once an improv comes to an end, if it seems at all promising it's usually worth involving the entire group in a discussion about its discoveries, its strengths, and the ways it could be developed subsequently, after which it is usually wise to adjust its given circumstances accordingly and return it to the floor.

As improvisations begin to evolve into scenes or other units, someone—the actors involved in each, a writer, the dramaturge (but ideally not the director)—needs to annotate and record them, usually giving each one a title (as a mnemonic) and recording what happens in it. This may or may not include text, and if it does, it may or may not involve crafting and refining that text to eliminate the kinds of pauses, approximations, and repetitions that are the inevitable residue of improvisations.

Similarly, you as director, a movement coach, or a choreographer might be involved in refining an improvisation's movement patterns, or indeed in choreographing movement for the evolving scene, eliminating improvisatory flab and crafting movements that are precise and efficient.

3. *Structuring*

In most devising processes, although these stages inevitably overlap and loop, analysis and embodiment, improvisation and annotation, are followed by some combination of either conscious or organic structuring. The dramaturgy of the performance builds, from this point, on the patterns, designs, shapes, and worlds identified earlier in the assembled resources, and internalized by the performers. It's your job as director/dramaturge to pay close attention to how these various elements manifest themselves in the work and consciously to shape them into a coherent, or artfully fragmented, whole.

Indeed at some point about two-thirds of the way through the process someone—the director, the dramaturge—usually begins to put charts or Post-it notes on the walls of the studio with the working titles of evolving scenes, beginning the process of sequencing and structuring a show.

In almost every case in this process there will be obvious groupings, evolving plots or subplots, interlinked or thematically related scenes, as well as a (hopefully small) group of scenes that don't seem to fit.

It's often best, once a preliminary discussion and negotiation of sequencing is complete, to revisit the scenes that initially don't seem to fit. Sometimes they genuinely don't and need to be cut (and sometimes this is a difficult decision). But often, once the larger shape of the show is becoming apparent, putting them back into circulation in studio can reveal their centrality; often, indeed, these scenes can become cornerstones or transformational points in the show once they have been tweaked and reintegrated into the evolving action.

It can also become clear at this stage that some of the scenes under development are redundant, performing similar or overlapping functions in the evolving trajectory of the show. At this point the scenes in question have to be merged, or some of them have to be trimmed or cut.

Finally, it can become apparent, sometimes quite late in the process, that there are gaps in the trajectory, missing scenes, beats, or moments that have to be invented. If these are small beats or bits of information they can be inserted through the normal course of rehearsals; if they are more major, extending to entire scenes or sequences, it's usually necessary to return to creation mode, to improvisations in studio that will serve, with the usual refinements, to bridge the gaps.

Eventually, through a series of negotiations, discussions, rearrangements, and reinventions, you'll find yourself as director performing the usual functions of rehearsing a show like any other, except that the company often feels greater ownership and greater commitment to the "product" than they sometimes do with pre-scripted work, and except that tech week should go more smoothly if you've been able to incorporate most or all elements of production into the process throughout.

INDEX

Ric Knowles works as a scholar, author, editor, director, and dramaturge. He is the author of several books, including *The Theatre of Form and the Production of Meaning*, *Reading the Material Theatre*, and *How Theatre Means*; past editor of *Canadian Theatre Review* and *Modern Drama*; and current editor of *Theatre Journal*. Ric is also general editor of the book series Critical Perspectives on Canadian Theatre in English and New Essays on Canadian Theatre, published by Playwrights Canada Press. He lives in Guelph, Ontario and is Professor of Theatre Studies at the University of Guelph.

Pat Flood is a theatre, film, and television designer and Past President of the Associated Designers of Canada. Her design work includes productions at the Blyth Festival; Theatre Calgary; Tarragon Theatre; Neptune Theatre, Halifax; Theatre New Brunswick; and the Gate Theatre in Dublin, Ireland. Film and television credits include *The Kids in the Hall*, *Fraggle Rock*, *Ararat*, and *Where the Truth Lies*. She is currently Associate Professor in the School of English and Theatre Studies at the University of Guelph.

First edition: September 2015.
Second printing: November 2016.
Printed and bound in Canada by Marquis Book Printing,
Montreal

Cover design by Christine Mangosing / CMANGO Design

PLAYWRIGHTS
CANADA PRESS

202-269 Richmond St. W.
Toronto, ON
M5V 1X1

416.703.0013
info@playwrightscanada.com
playwrightscanada.com

A bundled eBook edition is available
with the purchase of this print book.

CLEARLY PRINT YOUR NAME ABOVE IN UPPER CASE

Instructions to claim your eBook edition:
1. Download the BitLit app for Android or iOS
2. Write your name in **UPPER CASE** above
3. Use the BitLit app to submit a photo
4. Download your eBook to any device

RECYCLED
Paper made from
recycled material
FSC® C103567

Printed on Rolland Enviro, which contains 100% post-
consumer fiber, is ECOLOGO, Processed Chlorine Free,
Ancient Forest Friendly and FSC® certified
and is manufactured using renewable biogas energy.

PERMANENT   100%   BIO GAS
ENERGY

Ancient
Forest
Friendly™